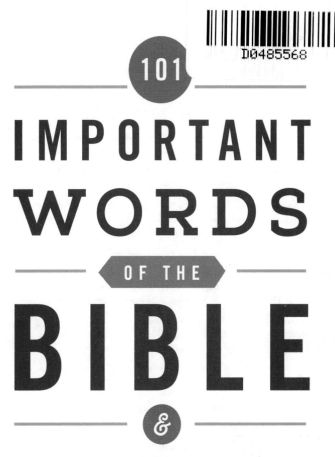

101
IMPORTANT
WORDS
OF THE
BIBLE

&

THE UNFORGETTABLE STORY THEY TELL

LEN WOODS

Our Daily Bread
Publishing™

Interior design by Rob Williams, InsideOutCreativeArts.com.

ISBN: 978-1-64070-011-6

Library of Congress Cataloging-in-Publication Data

Names: Woods, Len, author.

Title: 101 important words of the Bible : & the unforgettable story they tell / Len Woods.

Other titles: One hundred one important words of the Bible

Description: Grand Rapids, MI : Our Daily Bread Publishing, 2020. | Includes index. |
Summary: "101 key words can guide you to greater reverence for God's Story and a new
appreciation and love for studying the Word"-- Provided by publisher.

Identifiers: LCCN 2020009533 | ISBN 9781640700116 (paperback)

Subjects: LCSH: Bible--Criticism, interpretation, etc. | BISAC: RELIGION / Christian Life
/ Devotional | RELIGION / Biblical Meditations / General

Classification: LCC BS511.3 .W664 2020 | DDC 220.6--dc23

LC record available at https://lccn.loc.gov/2020009533

Printed in the United States of America

20 21 22 23 24 25 26 27 / 8 7 6 5 4 3 2

To Jan and Ellen, big sisters who loved me, looked out for me, and sometimes let me be in charge

CONTENTS

"And God spoke all these words"

—Exodus 20:1

INTRODUCTION

Making the Mummies Dance

By 1966, New York City's famed Metropolitan Museum of Art
had lost whatever pizzazz it ever possessed. Its collections
were stale and dated. Visiting exhibitions consisted mostly of ar-
cane works by obscure artists, known only to a few aficionados
and highbrows. With dismal attendance and declining revenues,
the Met was more like a mausoleum than a museum.

In 1967 the desperate powers-that-be turned to thirty-six-
year-old Thomas Hoving. As he took the reins of the Met, New
York Mayor John Lindsay told him, "Seems to me the place is dead.
But, Hoving, you'll make the mummies dance."

The tireless, innovative Hoving rolled up his sleeves. For the
next decade he poured himself into the task of revamping, re-
branding, and reintroducing the Met to a new generation. A bold
risk-taker and shrewd dealmaker, Hoving seized every possible
opportunity to create buzz. With the brashness and charm of a
Rhett Butler—and the marketing skill of a P. T. Barnum—he
solicited (and secured!) large donations from patrons. He then
splurged on exquisite, high-profile works of art. He updated the
aging Met facility—adding snazzy gift shops and elegant plazas.
Under Hoving's watch, the Met became the talk of the town. It
wasn't long before thousands of regular non-artsy people were
pouring each week through the museum's new Fifth Avenue en-
trance to gawk at all the Met's treasures.

The moral of the story? Get the mummies to dance and
you'll draw a crowd every single time.

• • •

Fast-forward to 2017. A nationwide survey conducted by Barna Group discovered the stunning truth that there's a Bible in roughly nine out of ten US households!

Yet when those same respondents were asked if they bothered to read the Bible even just *three to four times a year*, only half said yes. (About one-third admitted they *never* read the Bible.) Interestingly, roughly three out of five surveyed said they "wish they read the Bible more often." (Too bad the pollsters didn't ask, What's stopping you?)

It's head-scratching—Bibles everywhere we look—but few people take the time to explore them. Makes you wonder if the Good Book is viewed today the way New Yorkers viewed the Metropolitan Museum of Art in 1966. Perhaps the word on the streets is that the Bible is lifeless and irrelevant—something only a few weird, spiritual elites would ever find interesting. Maybe people tell pollsters they *want* to read the Bible—while secretly considering the Bible an out-of-date yawn-fest.

If all that's true, maybe it's time for the biblical equivalent of dancing mummies.

• • •

Let's go ahead and state the obvious. For many people—Christians included—the Bible is both intimidating and confusing.

Consider first its sheer size. All that tiny print on all those super thin pages. Admit it. It's unnerving! Depending on which translation you're reading from, an English Bible contains about 750,000 words (give or take 25,000).[*] To get some perspective, consider that Leo Tolstoy's epic novel *War and Peace* is a *mere*

---

[*] This figure doesn't count the apocryphal books included in Catholic Bibles or the added explanatory notes found in many popular study Bibles.

587,287 words! (Basically a pamphlet!) If it's true that most adults read between 200 and 300 words a minute, this means reading straight through the Bible would take the average person fifty to seventy hours!

And it's when people try to do that—read straight through the Bible like you would any other book—that they get confused. This is because, technically speaking, the Bible isn't a single book—it's a whole library of books, written long ago, over many centuries, by multiple authors. This is why the Bible doesn't read anything like a modern novel or a topical work of nonfiction.

Think about it this way: Imagine bumping around in your great-grandmother's attic one winter's day and discovering an immense scrapbook. You stare wide-eyed at those dusty, crinkly pages adorned with the faded photos of long-gone ancestors. In between those pages brown with age, some pack-rat relative has stuffed a trunk load of other documents. There are old birth and military records—and what seem like pages from a diary, written in elegant cursive. You shake your head at tattered death certificates and assorted legal papers—including obsolete property deeds and old wills. In the dim light, you find secret family recipes, fragile love letters, and postcards from long-ago vacations.

The Bible is something like *that*. It's an anthology of documents composed and collected by the ancient people of God. This hodgepodge of writings includes historical records, literary "snapshots" of old saints, long lists of laws, pages of prayers, assorted songs and sayings, sermons and stories. The Bible's got everything from genealogical records to building plans; census figures to private correspondence; racy poetry to strange, otherworldly prophecies about the future. And just as the old scrapbook in the attic tells the complicated story of a family, the holy scrapbook we call the Bible tells the remarkable story of the family of God.

• • •

The Bible is like the Metropolitan Museum of Art in this way: it's full of old and beautiful and priceless treasures. The Bible is unlike the Met in that it doesn't need anyone to come along and "breathe new life" into it.

Here's what most people don't realize: the Bible's ancient contents already throb with life! The apostle Paul observed, "All [that is, every word of] Scripture is God-breathed" (2 Timothy 3:16). The writer of Hebrews added, "The word of God is alive and powerful" (Hebrews 4:12 NLT).

Make the Bible come alive? The idea is laughable, like seeking to make a tornado windy, the Pacific Ocean wet. Instead, what we need is to stop what we're doing and pay attention to the way *the words of Scripture are already dancing with the truth of God!*

Scholars tell us the entire Bible was written using some 14,000 unique Hebrew and Greek words (plus a few in Aramaic). Strung together in various combinations, these words tell an astonishing story: why the world isn't the way God originally designed it to be, what God has done in Jesus—and is doing by His Spirit—to make all things new, and how taking His sacred words to heart can transform us—and the world.

Though *all* the words of Scripture are important for our spiritual understanding and worthy of attention, in these pages we'll spotlight only a hundred and one, at least one from each book of the Bible—Genesis to Revelation. A hundred and one God-breathed words that are pulsing with life—and with serious implications for our lives. In pausing to peek at and briefly ponder these verbs, nouns, names, and exclamations, we'll get a good overview of the timeless story of the Bible.

Are you ready to begin?

GOD

The generic name for the Bible's main character

In the beginning God created the heavens and the earth. (GENESIS 1:1)

The opening chapter of the Bible says nothing about neutrons, isotopes, or cosmic microwave backgrounds. In truth, Genesis 1 reads like a celebratory poem, not a science text. It simply states that before and behind all things ("the heavens and the earth") is a greater Cause. "In the beginning, God . . ."

This is the logical first stop on our 101-word trip through the Bible. The book of God begins with *God*.

• • •

God is a tiny word—with infinite implications. The Hebrew word is *elohim*, which is a generic name or title for deity (even pagan deities) in the Old Testament.

Interestingly, *elohim* is plural in form—even though we translate it singularly as "God" not "gods." Scholars suspect this is an ancient Jewish way of saying "the One we worship is not just a limited or singular majesty, but the sum total or fullness of *all* true majesty." Others see this plural noun in the light of later biblical revelation and theorize that this is a clever way of suggesting that the God of the Bible is a head-scratching tri-unity of divine persons: one

God, existing eternally as three distinct, coequal, coeternal persons—Father, Son, and Holy Spirit. (Try not to strain your brain.)

Later in the Bible, angelic beings (see Job 1:6) and even Israel's human rulers are called *elohim* (see Psalm 82:6), likely because they serve as God's representatives on earth.

• • •

A good story always begins by introducing the reader to the world of the story and to the protagonist, the main character.

So meet Elohim, your protagonist, the hero in this story of stories. Everything starts with God and revolves around Him.* Here at the start, all we know for sure is that God is a powerful Creator. In the opening chapters of Genesis, we get a sense of what Elohim wants—a beautiful world He can share with the creatures who are said to be made in His image.

• • •

The rest of the Bible reveals other fascinating names and titles for God. Here, however, it's Elohim, effortlessly speaking galaxies and gardenias, genes and jellyfish into existence.

For now, take a few moments to marvel at the wondrous world you inhabit. Any possibility the stunning complexity and beauty of the cosmos—and of *you*—could be the result of eons of time and blind chance? Only if you believe a tornado could smash into the hardware store in Wampum, Oklahoma, blow down the paint aisle, and leave something like the *Mona Lisa* on the back wall before exiting.

---

*This book will follow the biblical practice, and traditional custom, of using masculine pronouns— He, His, Him—in referring to God. This is not because God is thought to be "male" (in the same way we think of human masculinity). In truth, some biblical texts describe God in ways we might consider "feminine" (see, for example, Isaiah 49:15; 66:13; Hosea 13:8). The image of God in humanity is revealed as both "male and female" (Genesis 1:26–28).

MAKE

To design or craft with great skill

Let us make mankind in our image, in our likeness. (GENESIS 1:26)

You make your alarm clock stop squawking. You make coffee. You try to make yourself presentable before you make your way to work so that you can make hay while the sun shines. Why this incessant "making"? Because you, my friend, are a *maker*.

The opening sentence of the Bible reads, "In the beginning, God created the heavens and the earth." This famous statement about the origin of everything is followed by a short summary of God's creative activity (and the repetitive observation, "it was good... it was good... it was good"). Near the end of Genesis 1, we get to see the last item on the Almighty's ultimate to-do list: "Let us make mankind in our image, in our likeness" (Genesis 1:26).

• • •

The verb translated "make" here[*] means "to design, or fashion with great skill." (It's used similarly in Exodus 31:6 to describe the freakishly talented individuals who helped design the Jewish tabernacle; see chapter 8.) The use of this word is meant to help us see God as the cosmic Craftsman, the Artist par excellence.

---

[*]The common Hebrew word is `asah.

And the statement that humanity would be made *in God's image*? Gasp-worthy. The word translated "image" is "icon" in Greek. We've all seen an icon. It's a portrait, likeness, or representation of something or someone else—meaning, the triune God made the human race to represent himself.

• • •

Stunning, isn't it? You are the finite icon of an infinite God. I am a living, breathing work of art meant to resemble my Maker. This is the Bible's way of saying that we humans are God's pièce de résistance. He saved the best for last. No wonder God, after studying His pristine new creation one final time, *after* making human life, labeled it all not just "good" but "very good" (Genesis 1:31).

The point is unmissable: if we humans were made by the ultimate Maker to reflect and resemble Him, then *it is in our essential nature to make things.*

And thus all the imperfect people everywhere we look—in the pages of the Bible, in the next cubicle, in the bathroom mirror—making all manner of things. Plans and decisions, messes and mistakes, endless excuses. We make friends, make merry, make love, make babies. We make others miserable (or sad or angry or wary). Sadly, we sometimes make enemies. Thankfully, we have it within us to make amends and make up.

• • •

Here's the beautiful truth: made in the image of our Maker, WE are makers. God designed us with a godlike capacity to create. And God gives us time as a kind of workspace or laboratory in which to do our thing.

So, what will you make today? A meal? A memory? Art? A new friend? Peace with your past? Progress toward a goal? An effort to reach out and listen and help someone who's hurting?

The Bible reveals that we are makers, you and I. And when we make up our minds to seize the opportunities before us, we make the best of all things . . .

A difference.

3

DIE

To cease to be alive

You must not eat from the tree of the knowledge of good and evil,
for when you eat from it you will certainly die. (GENESIS 2:17)

According to ecology.com, about 200 people will pass away in the time it takes you to read this page (hopefully not you!). That's roughly 6,300 folks departing this life every hour, which comes to some 150,000 earthlings per day, and more than 53 million souls—slightly more than the populations of Florida and Texas put together—going to the Great Beyond each year.

Because the grim reality of the grim reaper makes us squirm, we use euphemisms. We speak of people "shuffling off this mortal coil" or "entering eternal rest." Yet when the Bible first broaches the subject of mortality—in just the second chapter—the language is blunt, straightforward, and euphemism-free.* God tells the first human, in essence, Try to find life and meaning apart from me, and you will surely die.

● ● ●

*The Bible does occasionally use euphemisms for death. It speaks of individuals who "go the way of all the earth" (see Joshua 23:14) and had "breathed [their] last" (see Genesis 35:18 and Mark 15:37) and are "gathered to [their] people" (see Genesis 25:8).

The Hebrew word translated "die" means exactly what we think: to stop living. In Genesis 2:17 it's an imperfect verb form paired back to back with an infinitive absolute of the same verb! Since you've forgotten all that fascinating grammar you crammed into your cranium back in high school, here's all that means: this is an *intense* declaration from God about the consequence of rejecting Him. We could translate it "dying, you will die."

On a practical level, death means *separation*. We know this tearful reality all too well. In death the soul exits the body. This personal separation leads to relational separation: survivors are left to mourn departed loved ones. In Genesis 2–3, we read about an even worse separation. Defying God is like unplugging from God. The result of sin is death in the spiritual sense.

● ● ●

Death as a consequence for sin is an entirely logical theological truth. What other outcome could there be when we separate ourselves from the holy One who is the essence of life and who first animated us with the mysterious "breath of life" (Genesis 2:7)? In the New Testament, the apostle Paul summarized this grimmest of realities this way, "Sin entered the world through one man, and death through sin, and in this way death came to all people, because all sinned" (Romans 5:12).

The rebellion in Paradise is beyond tragic. The first book of the Bible opens with life in all its pristine beauty and marvelous goodness. Eden is a deathless world, just as God meant for it to be. But sin comes crashing into the picture, and as a result, Genesis concludes with talk of embalming fluid, coffins, and burial plots.

● ● ●

In Genesis, death quickly moves from possibility (Genesis 2) to ugly reality (Genesis 3).

The good news, however, is that Genesis is only the beginning of God's great story. All has been lost, but all is not lost. The Almighty has a plan to put death to death.

Buckle up.

4

ABRAHAM

The patriarch of the Jewish people and
the father of all who believe

"Abraham believed God, and it was credited to him as righteousness,"
and he was called God's friend. (JAMES 2:23)

If we carved a "Mount Rushmore of Old Testament Greats,"
we'd make Abraham's face jut out prominently on the far left,
like George Washington's. Americans refer figuratively to our first
president as the "father of his country." But Abraham *literally* was
the father of his. And his story is undeniable proof of God's grace.

When introduced in Genesis 11, Abraham is seventy-five and
living in Ur, near the Persian Gulf (modern-day Iraq). He is almost certainly a worshiper of various Mesopotamian idols
(Joshua 24:2). He hasn't yet met the God of the Bible. At the time,
he is known as Abram, which means "exalted father." In one
of life's cruel ironies, the old guy is married to a woman (Sarai,
later known as Sarah) who can't have kids.

• • •

In a sudden and shocking display of goodness, the one true God
comes crashing into Abram's life with a suitcase full of outlandish
promises: In his old age, Abram will become the father of a great
nation! What's more, he will be blessed, his name will become

great, and his descendants will be a blessing to all peoples on earth (Genesis 12:1–3)!

But wait, there's more. God pledges a homeland (Genesis 12:6) to Abram. He promises to be his shield (Genesis 15:1) and then He changes Abram's name to *Abraham* (Genesis 17:5) which means "father of a multitude."

• • •

Talk about a name that fits—Abraham indeed becomes the father of a multitude. Not only father of the Jewish people, but also the patriarch of the Arab peoples (through his son Ishmael, whom he has with Hagar, Sarah's maid—see Genesis 16).

Spiritually speaking, Abraham becomes "the father of all who believe" (Romans 4:11). This is because when God said, "Go from your country (Genesis 12:1)," Abraham "obeyed and went, even though he did not know where he was going. By faith he made his home in the promised land" (Hebrews 11:8–9). When God assured the old man his descendants would outnumber the stars, he "believed the LORD, and the LORD counted him as righteous because of his faith" (Genesis 15:6 NLT).

• • •

Abraham's greatest descendant? That's easy: Jesus of Nazareth (Matthew 1:1). The New Testament declares that it's through Him—through Christ's perfect life, sacrificial death, and glorious resurrection—that we are able to enjoy "a right relationship with God" (Romans 4:13 NLT). And how do we get it? "It is given as a free gift. And we are all certain to receive it . . . if we have faith like Abraham's. For Abraham is the father of all who believe" (Romans 4:16 NLT).

Do you have a faith like Abraham's? More specifically, where in your life do you need to trust God today?

5

BLESS

To give what is good to another

Then the man said, "Let me go, for the dawn is breaking!" But Jacob said, "I will not let you go unless you bless me." (GENESIS 32:26 NLT)

It's as strange a Bible story as there is (Genesis 32:24–32). Jacob, the sketchy, shady grandson of Abraham, encounters a mysterious stranger—later said to be God himself! The two engage in a fierce, all-night wrestling match, during which a tenacious (or stubborn?) Jacob grunts, "I will not let you go unless you *bless* me." Just before sunrise, it's done. Jacob walks away with God's blessing, a new name, and a lifelong limp as a souvenir of the occasion.

• • •

When a group of Southern women see a fashion-challenged soul wearing white shoes after Labor Day, "Bless her heart!" is what they murmur to one another. Sneeze in a crowded room and chances are good someone will respond, "Bless you!"

The Hebrew verb translated "bless" is *barak*. It means to give good things to another. Most often in the Bible, God is depicted as the one doing the blessing. The clear implication is that we can (and should) petition the Almighty to pour out His favor on a loved one, a friend, a stranger, a marriage, or a venture meant to help others. When Jesus famously blessed the loaves and fish (Mark 6:41), it wasn't solely a prayer of thanks; it was also a request that His Father in heaven might take that meager amount of food, make much of it, and nourish the massive crowd before Him. And, of course, God did.

Occasionally, the Bible shows people approaching God not to seek a blessing from Him but rather to give one to Him. David, for example, urged himself repeatedly in Psalm 103 to "Bless the LORD, O my soul" (Psalm 103:1 NASB). This form of blessing—from creature to Creator—literally conveys the ideas of kneeling, adoring, or praising God. Those are some of the good things we can give back to God. We can bless our Maker by giving Him the glory and honor He deserves.

• • •

If the blessings we request from God are physical and material only—health and wealth—two things are true: First, our view of "divine blessings" is far too small. Second, we need to be asking for much more—immaterial riches like peace, joy, love, and patience.

Also, in all this "blessing business," we need to guard against self-centeredness. From beginning to end, the Bible says that God blesses His people so that they will turn around and bless others. We are meant to be conduits of the rich favor of God.

• • •

Perhaps like Jacob we should be wrestling with God over this whole notion of *blessing*. Are we grateful for His grace to us? Do we bless Him as He deserves—or is all the blessing in our lives flowing one way only? Do we freely pass on God's blessings: the truths we've learned, the resources He's given, the gifts and abilities He's dropped in our laps? Whom besides God can you bless today?

MOSES

Israel's great liberator and lawgiver

The LORD would speak to Moses face to face,
as one speaks to a friend. (EXODUS 33:11)

Remember that hypothetical "Mount Rushmore of Old Testament Greats" we mentioned a couple chapters back? If Abraham's face is carved on the far left, then next to him we have to add the mug of Moses.

Holy Moses—what a life! In infancy, Moses was nearly the victim of a genocidal Egyptian pharaoh—until the ruler's daughter saved him and took him as her own son.

He lived 120 years. Someone has observed that Moses spent his first forty years in the royal palace thinking he was somebody, his next forty years in the deserts of Midian realizing he was nobody, and his last forty years seeing what God Almighty can do through a nobody who obeys him. Indeed, the Bible gives exactly one chapter (Exodus 2) to Moses's first eighty years—but 135 chapters (Exodus 3–Deuteronomy 34) to his final forty years!

• • •

Pharaoh's daughter gave Moses his name. *Mosheh* is derived from the Hebrew verb that means to "draw out." Exodus 2:10 reveals she did this because she plucked him from the Nile River.*

At age forty, the adopted Moses—perhaps feeling guilty over his cushy life of royal privilege—tried to ease the suffering of his fellow Hebrews. His efforts backfired. He ended up fleeing Egypt and hunkering down in the deserts of Midian. There Moses consigned himself to a ho-hum life. He married and had a couple of kids. He tended sheep and probably figured his best days were behind him.

Only they weren't.

Moses got "Moses-ed" (that is, "drawn out") again! When he was *eighty*, Moses heard God call to him from the midst of a burning bush! That was the day the Lord plucked Moses from his dead-end life in Midian and sent him to "draw out" his captive countrymen from Egypt.

• • •

Truth be told, the name Moses doesn't matter a whole lot. But the *man* Moses—and his example—surely does. This reticent leader (see Exodus 3–4) courageously confronted the world's most powerful ruler. He guided the Israelites out of service to Pharaoh and into the freedom of serving God. He humbly (Numbers 12:3) shepherded the Israelites for forty exasperating years, then brought them to the edge of the promised land. When they sinned grievously, it was Moses who interceded for them. When Moses died, God officiated his private funeral (see Deuteronomy 34)!

• • •

---

*What was a baby doing in the Nile? When the paranoid pharaoh became concerned about the growing numbers of Hebrews in his land, he decreed that all these resident aliens throw their infant sons into the river. Moses's parents "sort of" obeyed, placing him in a floating waterproof basket instead (see Exodus 2:1–10), near the place where the pharaoh's daughter came to bathe.

If we could talk to Moses, odds are he'd tell us that the greatest miracle he ever saw—and he saw some doozies—was the miracle of God *drawing him out*: first, out of certain death as a baby, and later, out of a dull existence, in order to be His friend (Exodus 33:11) and to send him to help others.

The rest of the Bible indicates that's precisely what God wants to do in each of our lives: rescue us from death and then use us to rescue others.

LAW

The legal code (of instructions and prohibitions)
that God gave to Israel

The LORD said to Moses, "Come up to me on the mountain and stay here,
and I will give you the tablets of stone with the law and commandments
I have written for their instruction." (EXODUS 24:12)

When someone mentions the law of God, most of us think immediately of history's most famous list: the Ten Commandments. In truth, God's law is much more involved.

Jewish religious leaders over the centuries codified all the restrictions and requirements given to Moses by God at Sinai. The consensus tally is—you might want to sit down for this—613 laws: 365 don'ts and 248 mandates, or dos.

It's not quite the US tax code. Even so, it's pages and pages of rules.

• • •

Torah is the Hebrew word translated "law" in the Old Testament. Scholars tell us it comes from a root verb that means "to throw or cast." Think of a quarterback throwing a football into the area where he wants his receiver to run, and you're close to the idea.

Jewish people refer collectively to the first five books of the Bible as the Torah or the Law.* They further speak of the "Oral Torah," which consists of all the sayings, interpretations, and teachings of venerated rabbis and Jewish leaders down through the ages. (They see these explanations and insights as implicit in the written law given to Moses. All together,† they fill more than 6,000 pages.)

● ● ●

Why such a complicated system of law? And why so many regulations? In brief, here's what the Torah reveals:

1. God's absolute holiness.
2. God's desire for His redeemed people to live in God-honoring and world-blessing ways.

Leviticus 20:26 expresses these twin ideas succinctly: "You are to be holy to me because I, the LORD, am holy, and I have set you apart from the nations to be my own."

By carefully observing the legal and moral code given at Sinai, Israel was to be a light to the nations, showing the world how good it is to know and serve the one true God.

● ● ●

God's rules aren't arbitrary. They were all given to protect God's people from harm and to provide for them the most fulfilling life possible. However, the Bible both shows and states that the

---

*The first five books of the Bible are also called the *Pentateuch*. That word is derived from two Greek words: the word *penta*, which means "five," and *teuchos*, which means "scroll." When people speak of the Pentateuch, they are referring to Genesis, Exodus, Leviticus, Numbers, and Deuteronomy.

†Jews call the original written version of the oral law the Mishnah. They refer to the rabbinic discussions of this as the Gemara. Together the Mishnah and Gemara compose the Talmud.

exacting requirements of God's law are impossible for us to follow perfectly (Romans 3:20; Titus 3:5). No one can do it. Not even a devout Jew like the apostle Paul, who was fanatical about trying to keep the law of God. Even he was finally forced to admit that the real purpose of the law was only to serve as "our guardian until Christ came that we might be justified by faith" (Galatians 3:24).

Let God's law show you how holy God is. But then, instead of just trying to memorize and live out a boatload of rules, ask God's Holy Spirit to rule your heart and animate your life. That's the way to be holy and joy-filled. It's how to become the kind of person who causes others to wonder, "What makes him or her tick?"

TABERNACLE

The tent where God dwelled among the ancient Israelites
before they built their temple

Make this tabernacle and all its furnishings exactly like the pattern
I will show you. (Exodus 25:9)

The book of Genesis suggests there once was a time, however brief, when God's practice was to draw near His human creatures routinely in order to converse and commune intimately with them (see Genesis 2:7–3:9). Adam and Eve's sin changed all that.

The first couple was promptly banished from Paradise. And God, while remaining perfectly gracious and good to humanity, became—how shall we say it—less accessible. To be sure, He continued to speak to people and appear to them in dreams; however, such divine encounters were rare exceptions, not everyday occurrences.

In Moses's day, these sorts of numinous[*] visitations increased. In fact, God himself led the Hebrew people out of Egypt—via a massive cloud during daylight and a giant pillar of fire at night. Even so, God remained at a safe distance. Then, at Mount Sinai,

---

[*] *Numinous* is a term derived from the Latin word *numen* that means "divine will or power or nod." A numinous experience is one in which God signals His presence in an undeniable way.

in addition to the law, God gave the Hebrews detailed instructions for something called a *tabernacle*. There God promised to live— in their midst—and be their God!

• • •

The Hebrew word for *tabernacle* means "dwelling place," which for nomadic peoples was a tent.* Thus, the Greek word for *tabernacle* means literally "to live in a tent."

The idea conveyed through the word *tabernacle* is one of nearness, living close by, like the neighbors in the next campsite.

• • •

The ancient Jewish tabernacle—planned by God and built by artisans like Bezalel and Oholiab (see Exodus 25–31, 35–40)— was a basic "beta version" of the later Jewish temple. Essentially a big tent made out of animal skins, the tabernacle would function as Israel's portable worship center. In this rustic enclosure— that would need to be set up and taken down frequently— Moses's brother, Aaron, and others from their tribe would serve as the nation's priests. At this tabernacle, they would offer sacrifices to God.

Sure enough, when Moses and the people finished building and dedicating it, "the glory of the LORD filled the tabernacle" (Exodus 40:34). Imagine that: God condescending to dwell in a tent!

• • •

In the New Testament there's a related passage that can make your heart skip a beat. John 1:1–14 speaks of God becoming human and *tabernacling* among us: "The Word became flesh and made

---

*The Hebrew word is *mishkan*. The Greek word is *skenoō*.

his dwelling among us" (v. 14). When the writer, believed to be the apostle John, mentions "the Word," he is referencing Jesus of Nazareth. And if we dare to believe his testimony, everything changes. John's claim means God *isn't* aloof and distant. On the contrary, He came near. In the first century he "pitched his tent" among the Jewish people.

Think of that: had you lived in Jerusalem, in say, AD 29, you could have rubbed shoulders with God Almighty.

HOLY

Set apart from evil; morally perfect

I am the LORD, who brought you up out of Egypt to be your God;
therefore be holy, because I am holy. (LEVITICUS 11:45)

If any book of the Bible could use an image consultant, it's the book of Leviticus. People describe the third book of the Bible in odd ways, for example, "Leviticus is like brussels sprouts—probably good for me, but I tried it once, and, well, that was enough to last a lifetime." Or they sheepishly confess that Leviticus was where their read-through-the-Bible plan crashed and burned.

How tragic! The *first* book Jewish children used to study in synagogue classes* is the *last* bit of Scripture most Christians read.

Ignore Leviticus and you might miss one of the Bible's most crucial words: *holy*. Various forms of the word are found here more than 150 times! That's more mentions than in any other book in the Bible.

• • •

The literal and technical meaning of the term *holy* conveys the idea of separateness. To say that God is holy is to say that He is set

---

* According to Gordon. J. Wenham, *The Book of Leviticus*, New International Commentary on the Old Testament (Grand Rapids, MI: Eardmans, 1979), vii.

apart from all that is sinful and profane and imperfect. A holy thing or person is pure, unblemished, clean.

In effect, Leviticus was Israel's how-to manual for how unholy people could approach—and live with—a holy God. We could break down the book this way: Chapters 1–16 discuss dealing with sin so that one can approach a holy God. Chapters 17–27 talk about actually living with that God—that is, living holy lives and avoiding sin altogether.

• • •

Leviticus shows that treating God as holy means His people must approach Him with the gravest respect, soberly—not flippantly. Think of how a nuclear physicist treats radioactive material or a worker at the CDC handles a deadly virus. One careless moment can kill!

To be sure, Leviticus outlines a highly complicated system for approaching God. And to be honest, none of it makes much sense until you read the rest of the Bible—especially the New Testament.

• • •

Here's a worthwhile exercise. Read the book of Leviticus from start to finish (500 bonus points if you do it in one sitting). Circle or underline every reference to holiness. Then wrestle with this one question: since the divine command to the ancient Jews— "Be holy because I, the LORD your God, am holy" (Leviticus 19:2)—is repeated to New Testament believers—"Be holy in all you do" (1 Peter 1:15)—how does holiness need to be part of the story I am telling with my life today?

ATONEMENT

Reconciliation through a required payment

For the life of a creature is in the blood, and I have given it to you to make atonement for yourselves on the altar; it is the blood that makes atonement for one's life. (LEVITICUS 17:11)

One common—and entirely valid—criticism lobbed at the Bible by skeptics is that it is a violent book. People are constantly being bludgeoned or stabbed or flogged. Animals are repeatedly being slaughtered and sacrificed.

This raises unsettling questions: Why is the so-called Good Book so bloody? And what in the world does *atonement* mean?

● ● ●

The Hebrew root translated "atone" or "atonement" is found almost a hundred times in the Old Testament.[*] More than half of these occurrences are in Leviticus.

Since the word is used in Genesis 6:14 to describe how Noah slathered his newly built ark with gooey pitch, the word can mean "to cover or smear." Some point to this and say that in the same way the pitch covered Noah's ark and provided protection against

---

[*]The Hebrew root word is *kapar*.

the deadly flood waters, so the blood of an atoning sacrifice can "cover" a sinner, blot out his or her transgressions, and provide safety from divine judgment. In other words, atonement results in forgiveness.

In a broad sense, *atonement* means "reconciliation through a necessary payment." We all know how this works. In a kidnapping case, a ransom is offered in exchange for the person being held. In a legal court, a fine is paid to compensate for the wrong one has done. In Leviticus, an atoning sacrifice functioned as a substitute for the one making the offering.

Always, the end goal is reconciliation. That's actually the original meaning of our English word *atonement*: "the state of being at one with" (that is, at one with a person you were previously estranged from or at odds with).

•   •   •

In Leviticus, God reveals that atonement (being restored to a right relationship with Him) comes only through *sacrifices* and *offerings*. (In fact, these related words are found more than three hundred times in the book!)

And now you know why for centuries, countless bulls, goats, rams, sheep, and birds served as substitutes for countless sinners—their blood spilled and splattered on an altar, so that a guilty person's life might be spared.

To modern sensibilities, this system of blood sacrifice seems primitive, savage, unfair. Perhaps the degree to which we are embarrassed or outraged by the idea of atonement is directly tied to how much we've trivialized two realities: the holiness of God and the horror of sin.

•   •   •

The good news announced by the New Testament writers is that God sent His Son to be the ultimate, once-and-for-all sacrifice for sin (Hebrews 9:26–28). "Look," John the Baptist exclaimed, when he saw Jesus coming toward him, "the Lamb of God, who takes away the sin of the world!" (John 1:29).

Sure enough, when Jesus hung on the cross and yelled with His dying breath, "It is finished!" (John 19:30), he was talking about atonement. He was proclaiming the truth that no more sacrifices would ever need to be made. Atonement for sin was finished.

It was done forever.

PRIEST

A spiritual leader who stands in the gap between
a holy God and sinful people

The priests are to perform my service in such a way that they do not
become guilty and die for treating it with contempt. I am the LORD,
who makes them holy. (LEVITICUS 22:9)

In 2018, the Gallup organization researched the most and least trusted professions. "Clergy" received high marks from just 37 percent of those polled. (In 1985, this figure was 67 percent!) The silver lining—if there is one—is that religious professionals are still trusted more than car salespeople and members of Congress.

Sadly, even though many priests and ministers are good-hearted, we will always have a few bad apples. And even the really good priests and clergy members have off-days.

All except for One.

• • •

When God established Israel's religious system, He assigned one of its twelve tribes—the Levites—the 24-7 task of taking care of the tabernacle (Numbers 1:47–54). From the same tribe,

He called Aaron—the brother of Moses—and his family to serve as priests.* This was a hugely important role.

In ancient Israel, priests were the ones who represented God to the people. Their job description included blessing the people (Numbers 6:22–27), teaching the law of God (2 Chronicles 17:7–9), and sometimes acting as judges in legal matters (2 Chronicles 19:8–10).

Priests also represented people before God. They offered sacrifices on their behalf. Once a year, Israel's high priest would go trembling into the innermost part of the tabernacle, by himself, to sprinkle the blood of a "national" sacrifice onto the "mercy seat"—the lid of the holy, gold-covered box known as the ark of the covenant. The high priest did this to atone for the sins of all God's people, including his own.

• • •

In the first century, the Jewish followers of Jesus made a remarkable claim. They preached that by freely offering His life on the cross, Christ made a once-and-for-all atoning sacrifice for the sins of the whole world (Romans 3:25; 1 Corinthians 5:7). As such, they insisted, He was the ultimate high priest making the ultimate sacrifice. By this act He secured eternal forgiveness for all who would put their faith in Him.

One of Christ's followers—the apostle Paul—insisted that as a result of Jesus's sacrifice, *all* believers can now approach God directly (Ephesians 2:18). Almost as staggering is the apostle Peter's claim that *we* are all now priests (1 Peter 2:5), intermediaries between a God who loves the world and a world that desperately needs to be reconciled to God.

---

*The Hebrew words translated "priest" and "to serve as a priest," *kohen* and *kahan*, respectively, are found almost two hundred times in Leviticus, Israel's comprehensive "how-to" worship guide.

• • •

Let's be who the Bible says we are. Let's be priests today, approaching God without fear (Hebrews 4:16), bringing the spiritual needs of others to Him, and telling others of His love.

And where we fail in our role as priests, let's seek forgiveness from those we wrong and trust more deeply in Jesus, our great high priest, who never failed and never will.

REBEL

To willfully defy or revolt against authority,
in hopes of overthrowing it

Only do not rebel against the LORD.
And do not be afraid of the people of the land. (NUMBERS 14:9)

After all the exacting laws of Exodus and all the bloody offerings of Leviticus, many people shut the Bible.

Good grief! they think. God actually told the Israelites to create a special place where a bunch of priests could offer bloody sacrifices nonstop? Just because people sometimes make mistakes? Seriously?

Not quite.

• • •

If humanity's worst offense was an occasional honest mistake, then, yes, the Old Testament sacrificial system is over-the-top excessive. However, the Bible shows that we are guilty of much worse than periodic, inadvertent blunders.

Case in point: After leaving Mount Sinai, God led the Israelites to the border of Canaan, the land He had promised to give Abraham's descendants (see Genesis 17:7–8). But rather than take

God at His word and enter the land, the people had a collective panic attack. Fearful of the Canaanites, the Israelites balked. Two of the nation's leaders, Joshua and Caleb, begged the people to reconsider, "Do not rebel against the LORD," they cried (Joshua 22:19).

Rebel is a strong verb.* It means to willfully resist an authority or even to try to overthrow that authority. A mistake? A blunder? No, this is carefully considered defiance. *Rebel* is often used in the Old Testament alongside other strong synonyms for the word *sin*—the verbs to disobey (Nehemiah 9:26), to break faith (Joshua 22:16), to turn against (2 Kings 24:1), and to transgress (Ezekiel 2:3 NASB).

• • •

What can we say? Rebelling isn't a once-in-a-blue-moon occurrence. It's our default predisposition! The reason God has to make such a big deal over our sin? Behind our daily acts of defiance and disobedience is a treasonous desire to carry out a coup. We rebel against God's rule daily in premeditated decisions big and small. And it's not just that we want God to leave us alone. *We* want to be in charge. *We* want to make the rules.

C. S. Lewis explained human nature succinctly in his spiritual classic, *Mere Christianity*: "Fallen man is not simply an imperfect creature who needs improvement: he is a rebel who must lay down his arms."†

• • •

There are all sorts of things in life we ought to be rebelling against: injustice (and the systems and laws that perpetuate it), apathy, selfishness, corruption (especially apathy, selfishness, and corruption in our own hearts).

Rebel is *mārad* in Hebrew.
†C. S. Lewis, *Mere Christianity* (New York: HarperCollins, 1952/2001), 56.

Rebelling against God—that's a different story altogether, an eternally serious matter. To piggyback on Lewis's statement: Have you laid down your arms? Are you still fighting God for control of some aspect of life?

CLING

To hold fast to someone or something

You shall follow the LORD your God and fear Him;
and you shall keep His commandments, listen to His voice,
serve Him, and cling to Him.
(DEUTERONOMY 13:4 NASB)

The consequences of Israel's rebellion against God (see previous chapter) at the border of Canaan were dire. The Bible shows the people of God trudging about the dusty desert south of Canaan in a kind of national, forty-year time-out. Four decades of attending funerals—more than enough time to ponder their collective poor choice.

Their wandering ended in Moab, just east of the Jordan River. There, as this new generation of Israelites prepared to enter the promised land, Moses gave a series of messages. These addresses were equal parts history lesson, sermon, and pep talk. Among those last words was a plea to do the very opposite of rebel.

"Cling to God," the old liberator and lawgiver urged.

• • •

Cling is one of the most vivid words in the Old Testament.* It means "to stick to, or stay close to; to adhere, join with, fasten securely, bind together." Think of this as the Hebrew "glue" word.

The Bible uses it to refer to a lingering disease one can't shake, a waistband tied snugly around the midsection, a warrior holding on to a sword for dear life, a swollen tongue sticking to the roof of the mouth. It's also the word used to describe God's design for marriage in Genesis 2:24: "a man . . . *united* to his wife."

The rare and beautiful ideas communicated in the word *cling* are inseparability, commitment, devotion, and affection.

● ● ●

Moses was essentially telling all those young Jewish whippersnappers, "When you go into the promised land, hang on to God desperately, like a starving dog hanging on to a bone. Cling to God like your lives depend on it. Because in fact, your lives do."

Some bristle at such a thought. "*Cling*? That's what weak and needy people do!"

In truth, clinging is what *all* people do. Each of us latches on fiercely to some object, belief, cause, activity, or person that we assume will make us happy. Granted, some people are serial clingers. That is, they switch allegiances like a seventh-grade girl changes clothes, thinking, *If this attachment doesn't satisfy or save me, I'll grab ahold of another.*

But make no mistake: everybody clings to *something*.

● ● ●

What are you clinging to at this point in your life? What are your abiding commitments? Is your devotion to God "till death do you

---

** *Cling* is *dabaq* in Hebrew. (If you ever win big bucks on the game show *Jeopardy!* because you learned that fact here, I expect you to at least buy me a cup of coffee.)*

part," or do you follow Him most days the way most of us follow celebrities and situations on social media? Only in fits and spurts?

Why not take Moses's advice to heart? And when you do, realize that the One you're clinging to is already holding you (Psalm 63:8)!

14

REMEMBER

To purposely call to mind information
that is true and valuable

Remember that you were slaves in Egypt and the LORD your
God redeemed you. That is why I give you this command today.

(DEUTERONOMY 15:15)

You bump into a former coworker on the cereal aisle. You worked down the hall from her for almost *five* years—but you can't recall her name until you get to the frozen foods section. How embarrassing!

And disturbing. You think of your neighbor with Alzheimer's—he can't remember his daughter's name or how to put on a shirt. Suddenly you have the urge to work crossword puzzles and eat foods believed to stave off dementia.

While you're at it, you might also want to fight against *spiritual* dementia.

• • •

The Hebrew word translated "remember" means "to recall" (information or events) or "to summon to one's mind" (facts that are known to be true).[*] Hence biblical remembering is an intentional

---

[*] *Zakar* is the Hebrew word translated "remember."

act—not an unconscious, haphazard thing. It isn't hoping that memories and facts might somehow spring to mind—it's deliberately bringing them to mind.

The book of Deuteronomy is all about remembering. When God informed Moses that he wouldn't be leading the Israelites into the promised land, the revered leader starting acting like a nervous dad dropping his kids off at college. *Sixteen* times he told them to *remember* key moments from their history or important divine commands! And just in case any of them were tuning out all his reminders to *remember*, Moses shrewdly employed another phrase: urging them time and time again *not to forget*.

• • •

Why aren't we better remember-ers? The field of neuroscience suggests two possibilities.

We lose some memories because we simply don't access them often enough to keep them vivid. Think of writing something in the sand at the beach. Get distracted, look away, and before you know it, the waves will have washed away your words. In a similar way, without diligent efforts at preservation, our memories fade. This is why Moses begged the Israelites to be careful lest the things "your eyes have seen . . . fade from your heart" (Deuteronomy 4:9).

A second reason we forget is because our memories get overwritten by other information (or misinformation). Think of an eyewitness to a crime who is first grilled by detectives, then subtly manipulated and "coached" by an overeager district attorney, then befuddled by a slick defense attorney. Subjected to a steady stream of suggestive spin, dizzy from all the competing narratives he keeps hearing, our eyewitness may eventually forget what actually transpired. In time he may find himself "remembering" things that never occurred!

• • •

A wise old saint once observed that the Bible only contains about eight big ideas—and God just keeps repeating them over and over.*

Therein lies the value of returning to the Bible again and again. Not to win brownie points with God but to summon to our minds (and to review) the things that are True with a capital T.

---

*I'd state the Bible's big ideas this way: (1) There is a God. (2) He is glorious and good. (3) We are rebels who resist God and run from Him. (4) God sent His Son Jesus Christ to seek and save us. (5) We live—truly live—only by faith. (6) There's more to life than just this life. (7) God designed us to live in community. (8) Because God is in charge, all will be well.

LAND

A patch of ground; in the Bible often a reference
to the territory promised Abraham

Remember what Moses, the servant of the LORD, commanded you:
"The LORD your God is giving you a place of rest. He has given you this land."
(JOSHUA 1:13 NLT)

If you asked people to list the nouns used most frequently in the Bible, most would guess *Lord* and *God*. Few, if any, would mention the word *land*.

And yet *land* is the twelfth most common noun in the Bible!* It's found more times than names like *Jesus* and *Jerusalem* and words like *heart* and *soul*, *love* and *law*.

Who knew that real estate is such a big Bible topic?

• • •

The Hebrew word most often translated "land" in the Old Testament is derived from a word that means "to be firm."† Sometimes the word is rendered "earth" or "ground" (as in plain old dirt). Usually the word refers to a specific patch of land—the much-disputed

---

* According to King James Bible Online (www.kingjamesbibleonline.org).
† It's *'erets*.

and desired territory known variously as Canaan, the land of Israel, "the land flowing with milk and honey" (Exodus 33:3), the Jewish homeland, Zion, and Palestine.

In multiple places, the Bible discusses the land stretching from "the Wadi of Egypt to the great river, the Euphrates" (Genesis 15:18). This general area is the homeland promised to the Jewish patriarch Abraham: "And I will give the entire land of Canaan, where you now live as a foreigner, to you and your descendants. It will be their possession forever, and I will be their God" (Genesis 17:8 NLT).

• • •

For people who'd spent centuries in Egyptian bondage and decades more wandering the wilderness regions south of Canaan, God's promise of a good land was a dream come true. Crossing the Jordan River under the leadership of Joshua (see Joshua 3–5), the Israelites were finally in a place where they could put down roots.

God made it clear to them that all real estate everywhere ("the earth . . . and everything in it"—see Psalm 24:1) ultimately belongs to him. But even when we don't actually own land, we can appreciate the power of place. We are physical, flesh-and-blood creatures, who live in space and time. Our spirituality is inevitably linked to geography.

• • •

In her epic novel *Gone with the Wind*, novelist Margaret Mitchell had one of her characters say that land is the only thing in the world worth fighting and dying for, because "it's the only thing that lasts."

The Bible takes a different view about the permanence of land. It reveals a coming day when this old earth will actually be gone with the wind—as in, replaced by a "new earth."

In the end it's not particular parcels of real estate that matter most, but rather what God does in our hearts while we are in those places.

In what places have you had powerful encounters with God? What special chunks of land carry your best spiritual memories?

REST

A settled, favorable state in which one can find restoration

And now the LORD your God has given rest.

(JOSHUA 22:4 NASB)

Our language has some great words—few as beguiling as *rest*. Astonishing, isn't it, how merely hearing that word can send us into a (day)dream state? The mind imagines . . .

- A cabana on a tropical island surrounded by sapphire blue water.
- A good book . . . a big leather chair by a fire . . . a snowy day off.
- A baby who's finally given up his fierce fight against Mr. Sandman. Except for the infant's chest barely moving up and down, absolute stillness. Only breath.

● ● ●

It's doubtful that those Jewish tribes admiring their new digs in the promised land had much experience with true *rest*. All those years in the desert—constantly on the move. Followed by all that hard work of driving out Canaan's not-so-neighborly occupants.

The rest God offered Israel conveys the ideas of stopping and settling in.* After the tumultuous flood, Noah's ark came to rest (there's the word) on "the mountains of Ararat" (Genesis 8:4). The word also suggests peacefulness, thus the Old Testament references to sacrifices giving off a *soothing* (there's the word again) aroma.

To be at rest is to be in a place of peace and stillness, free from worry, full of joy (Isaiah 14:7).

● ● ●

Biblical rest is cessation—from toil and strain, from needing to figure everything out, from feeling like it's all on you to salvage things. Rest is going off duty. It's rooted in trust, in the conviction that God sees and cares, protects and provides. Rest is the comfort of knowing that when we're asleep, the Almighty is awake.

Biblical rest is also surrender. It's waving the proverbial white flag and saying, "I'm laying down my weapons in my private war against life, my ceaseless efforts to control outcomes and people."

And when we enter into such rest? We find that it is restorative. Rest revives and reenergizes us. Afterward we're renewed and replenished.

● ● ●

God designed the world with a work-life rhythm built right in. One day in seven—called the Sabbath (see Genesis 2:2–3; Deuteronomy 5:13–15)—is earmarked for stopping, unplugging, retreating, and remembering. Do you set aside a day a week to simply rest?

If, as you ponder this whole topic of rest, you hear yourself sigh, that's almost certainly an indicator of un-rest. You are likely rest-less.

---

*The Hebrew word for *rest* is *nuwach*.

The good news? You don't have to stay that way. Hear the invitation of Jesus: "Come to me, all you who are weary and burdened, and I will give you rest. Take my yoke upon you and learn from me, for I am gentle and humble in heart, and you will find rest for your souls" (Matthew 11:28–29).

JUDGES

The twelve individuals—after Joshua and before the time of the monarchy—God used to rescue and govern the fledgling, fickle nation of Israel

Then the LORD raised up judges, who saved them out of the hands of these raiders. (JUDGES 2:16)

When the legendary Moses died, Joshua was the guy tapped by God to assume command. Under his able leadership the people of God subdued the Canaanite tribes and settled in the promised land. As long as Joshua lived, "the people served the LORD" (Judges 2:7). But soon after his death, "the Israelites . . . forsook the LORD. . . . They followed and worshiped various gods of the peoples around them. . . . The LORD gave them into the hands of raiders who plundered them" (Judges 2:11–14).

Enter the judges.

• • •

If you're picturing robe-wearing, gavel-waving men and women, who say things like "habeas corpus" and "overruled!" think again. These judges weren't sitting around writing legal opinions. They were handpicked by God to bring judgment on Israel's enemies!

In case you forgot—or never knew—this period in Israel's history was chaotic. (Think the Wild Wild West.) The writer of the book of Judges put it this way:"In those days Israel had no king; everyone did as they saw fit" (Judges 21:25).

Given this "whatever" mind-set, it's not surprising that a grim national cycle kept repeating itself. The people *of* God would turn away *from* God. In order to "wake them up," God would permit a neighboring nation to invade and wreak havoc. When the Israelites got weary of such oppression, they would cry out to God for rescue. Mercifully, God would then send a judge to get His people out of their latest jam.

These men—and at least one woman—were first and foremost military heroes. Often they were dashing and charismatic. (Think William Wallace in *Braveheart*.) They led uprisings to drive out Israel's oppressors. In times of peace they functioned as civic leaders, offering a bit a structure to an out-of-control culture.

• • •

When we think of the biblical judges, two stunning truths ought to come to mind. One, God is merciful. That is to say, "he does not treat us as our sins deserve" (Psalm 103:10). He forgives us and rides to our rescue, over and over again. Two, God uses flawed people. There's no other way to say it—the judges had serious issues. Gideon seemed to battle an almost crippling fear. Samson may have been a sex addict. Jephthah was over-the-top impulsive. Thankfully, God is bigger than our flaws and failings.

• • •

Two questions are worth pondering:

1. If the Old Testament judges were just regular people empowered by God to lead others to freedom, who are the "judges" God has used most powerfully in your life? Have you ever thanked them for the way they have impacted you?

2. Instead of being a judge today in the modern sense of the word—that is, critiquing and condemning others—how can you be a judge who helps others find freedom?

KINSMAN-REDEEMER

A near relative who acts to redeem his kin from trouble

Then the women of the town said to Naomi, "Praise the LORD,
who has now provided a redeemer for your family!" (RUTH 4:14 NLT)

Reporter: Off the record—how exactly did you locate the bomb?
FBI Agent: If I told you that, I'd have to kill you.

Reporter: In that case, would you mind telling my mother-in-law?

There's a reason in-law jokes are a staple of stand-up Comedians. We know—from firsthand experience—that it's hard to bring new personalities into a family and keep the peace.

And yet there's a story in the Bible that shatters all our in-law stereotypes—*and* introduces us to an astonishing word. It's the story of Ruth. The word is the Hebrew *go'el*, translated variously as "redeemer" (NASB, ESV, and NLT), "kinsman" (KJV), or "guardian-redeemer" (NIV).

• • •

Against the dark backdrop of the time of the judges, the story of Ruth sparkles like a diamond. Two freshly widowed women—Naomi, a mother-in-law, and Ruth, her daughter-in-law—from different countries and cultures, forged an unlikely bond. Still mourning the loss of their husbands, they returned from Moab to lawless Israel to try to scratch out an existence.

In the providence of God, Ruth bumped into a wealthy, older gentleman named Boaz. He "just happened" to be one of Naomi's in-laws! Boaz provided food and security for the impoverished, vulnerable women. But that's not all. He also took on the noble responsibility of acting as a *go'el*. In this capacity—as the closest willing relative—he stood up legally for Naomi and Ruth. He pulled out his checkbook and bought back the land that formerly belonged to Naomi's husband.* Then, in a very odd and ancient Hebrew way, he essentially said to Ruth, "I know I'm getting long in the tooth, but if you'd have me, I'd love to make you my bride!"

A short time later, the two were saying, "I do." Not long after that, Naomi was holding her newborn grandson, Obed—who ended up being the grandfather of King David.

• • •

The story of Ruth is more than a heart-warming, 3,100-year-old Hallmark movie plot. To be sure, it offers some great lessons in faithfulness and sacrificial love. But maybe the biggest take-away is that word *go'el*.

Bible scholars note how the actions of Boaz in the Old Testament foreshadow the actions of Jesus in the New Testament. As an outsider, Ruth had no claim to any sort of blessing. And yet Boaz looked on her with compassion and paid a great price to redeem and marry her.

---

*See Leviticus 25 for the laws governing this practice of acting as a kinsman-redeemer.

Had Boaz not taken these steps, he'd literally have been Ruthless. Because he took them, King David was eventually born, and centuries after him, King Jesus. Go figure—a redeemer in the Old Testament resulted in the coming of the ultimate Redeemer.

• • •

If you've never read it, take a few minutes to check out the great story of Ruth. It features some bizarre cultural customs but nothing as outlandish or stunning as this truth:

God sent His own Son to be our *go'el*.

PROPHET

One chosen by God to deliver divine messages

And all Israel from Dan to Beersheba recognized that Samuel was attested as a prophet of the LORD. (1 SAMUEL 3:20)

If you think Israel's priests had a hard and thankless job, consider the Old Testament prophets.

Maybe if we put our heads together, we could come up with another group that was more misunderstood and more mistreated. Right now, it's hard to imagine what group that might be.

• • •

The word translated "prophet" refers to one authorized to be God's mouthpiece.* Abraham is the first person in the Bible called a prophet (Genesis 20:7). Moses was one (Deuteronomy 18:15; 34:10). So was his sister, Miriam (Exodus 15:20). Samuel was another.

Both men and women assumed prophetic roles. Some prophets (like Elijah in 1 Kings and Huldah in 2 Kings 22) communicated

---

*The word translated "prophet" in the Old Testament is the Hebrew *nabi*. Scholars can't agree on the etymology of the word. They don't know if it came from Hebrew, Arabic, Akkadian, or some other Semitic language.

their divine messages orally. Others (like Isaiah and Jeremiah) wrote down for posterity the things God instructed them to say.

We typically think of prophets as people who revealed events far in advance. In actuality, predicting the future (foretelling) was only one part of their job description. Many prophets stayed busy simply preaching God's truth (forth-telling). That is to say, they spoke blunt messages from God about keeping the law and caring for the poor. These pronouncements were often warnings to get in line—or else. Thus a big part of a prophet's emphasis on the future was delivering messages like, "If you don't start doing right *today*, you're going to deeply regret it *in days to come*."

However, not every prophetic message was stern. Often the prophets shared comforting messages with their discouraged listeners. The prophet Jeremiah, far from being an angry guy, was sometimes known as the weeping prophet.

The Bible also warns repeatedly about looking out for false prophets—people who claim to have a message from God but are really just spouting their own ideas (Matthew 7:15; Mark 13:22).

• • •

Some see the prophets as the original "social justice warriors." Others see them as a band of spiritual "performance artists." This is due to the odd things God often asked His spokespeople to do in order to drive their messages home. Isaiah had to walk around in his birthday suit (Isaiah 20:2–4). Jeremiah wore a farming implement around his neck (Jeremiah 27). Ezekiel was told to cook his food over human excrement (Ezekiel 4:12). Hosea was commanded to marry an immoral woman (Hosea 1:2).

Say what you want about the prophets—they were instructed to do some really hard and bizarre things. In almost every case, they gulped and did exactly as they were told.

• • •

For the most part, the prophets were ignored, scorned, beaten, and even martyred. They had a message to give and they gave it.

We may not envy the lives the prophets had, but wouldn't it be something if we had their hearts?

KING

One who exercises the functions of a monarch, governing, leading, and protecting a people

They said to him, "You are old, and your sons do not follow your ways; now appoint a king to lead us, such as all the other nations have."

(1 SAMUEL 8:5)

As of early 2019, there were fewer than thirty monarchies left in the world.

In Japan, they use the old classic title *emperor*. In Kuwait, it's *emir*. Liechtenstein and Monaco go with the understated *prince*—which may explain why Luxembourg decided on the upscale *grand duke*.

Citizens of Brunei call their monarch the *sultan*. Malaysia—obviously thinking, *We can do better than THAT!*—settled on *Yang di-Pertuan Agong,* which means "he who is made lord."

In the earliest years of ancient Israel, the leader of the nation was known as Yahweh (that is, He who already *is* LORD and doesn't need anyone to *make* Him Lord). The nation began as an actual theocracy, ruled directly by God, through spokesmen called prophets. But when the prophet Samuel was getting close to retirement age, a group of leaders approached him and made a bold request: we want a human king like all our neighbors.

• • •

The Hebrew word translated into English as "king" is *melek*. It's one of the most frequently found words in the Bible (occurring close to 3,000 times). *Melek* is related to the verb *malak*, which means "to reign." A king is one who exercises authority, one who rules.

Israel's experiment in monarchy was a good example of "be careful what you ask for." The nation's first king was Saul, a tall, good-looking guy who clearly cared more about public perception than he did about God's opinion.

David (see chapter 21) followed Saul as king, and even though he had a giant heart for God, he also had big feet of clay. His forty-year reign ended up being marked by stunning accomplishments—and spectacular scandal. David was succeeded by his son Solomon, who did the opposite of what most people do. Instead of getting wiser with age, Solomon began his reign as the wisest man on earth—then got progressively more foolish with each passing year.

• • •

Israel had other kings—a few good ones, the majority of them forgettable, or worse, regrettable. But the great truth the Israelites had a hard time remembering was that even when they had a human leader who wore a crown and waved a scepter from a fancy throne, God was their true, ultimate king. Multiple Bible verses say some version of this: "For the LORD Most High is awesome, the great King over all the earth" (Psalm 47:2).

• • •

As you read historical accounts of brutal potentates or watch online news reports about contemporary dictators, it's good to remember the one the Bible calls the King of the earth.

And while we're at it, it's also good to ask this question: "Is the King above all other kings, the true king of *my* heart?"

DAVID

The passionate shepherd-king of ancient Israel

David and all Israel were celebrating with all their might before the LORD.

(2 SAMUEL 6:5)

We could argue till the end of time about who deserves the fourth spot on our hypothetical "Mount Rushmore of Old Testament Greats." But there's no debate about the third member of our elite group. Next to Abraham and Moses, we're chiseling the face of David.

David is a towering figure in Scripture. In fact, in the NIV translation of the Bible, there are 1,009 mentions of *David*. Compare that to 924 mentions of *Jesus* (or *Jesus Christ* or *Christ*).

• • •

Some scholars think the name David may come from a Hebrew word that means "beloved." Others wonder if it's derived from an ancient Near Eastern word that means "leader." Who's right? No one knows for sure.

What we *do* know is that David was from the tribe of Judah and that he lived life full throttle. As a young boy, he fiercely protected his father's flocks—to the point of dispatching any lions and bears with predatory intentions (1 Samuel 17:34–37).

When he was a teenager, David heard Goliath taunting Israel's God—and went ballistic. Literally. You remember the story: With a single flip of his slingshot, David took down the Philistine behemoth—and became a national sensation and, in time, Israel's king.

David's love for God was over-the-moon obvious. Don't believe it? Check out the Psalms—he wrote about half of them—and see for yourself. Or simply watch David as the ark of God is finally brought back to Jerusalem (see 2 Samuel 6). He's the one dancing wildly and unashamedly at the head of the procession. (We've seen fraternity guys celebrate like this—except in David's case, he was drunk on pure, 200-proof joy.)

David's life was marked by overwhelming spiritual passion. However, there were other moments when powerful fleshly temptations got the best of him. The most sickening example? The time the man after God's own heart (1 Samuel 13:14) became the man after his general's own wife (2 Samuel 11–12).

• • •

The man David matters *historically* because of the remarkable way he ruled. With God's blessing, he defeated Israel's many enemies and led the nation to unprecedented security. Ezra summed up his kingship this way: "David reigned over all Israel, doing what was just and right for all his people" (2 Samuel 8:15).

This "sweet psalmist of Israel" (2 Samuel 23:1 NLT) matters *spiritually* because he gave the people of God through the ages a kind of soundtrack for life and faith.

David matters *ultimately* because in those psalms, he foretold the same future that the Old Testament prophets saw: one day another king from the tribe of Judah would come and sit on David's throne and rule forever with perfect passion.

• • •

You owe it to yourself to read at least three different psalms of David. For starters try Psalm 13—about trusting God when you're in trouble; Psalm 32—about what to do when you're reeling with guilt; and Psalm 103—about remembering God's true nature.

TEMPLE

The dwelling place of God on earth where people
came to pray and offer sacrifices

So Solomon built the temple and completed it. (1 Kings 6:14)

Anybody who has ever worshiped at a rustic outdoor pavilion
and at an ornate cathedral can relate to how the Israelites
must have felt when they said farewell to their modest old tabernacle (see chapter 8) and hello to their shiny new temple.

The tabernacle, from the time of Moses, was a portable structure—essentially a deluxe tent. The temple, on the other hand,
was constructed during the reign of King Solomon. It was situated
high on Mount Moriah in Jerusalem (2 Chronicles 3:1) and built
with the finest Tyrian lumber and Lebanese stone (see 1 Kings 5).

From a human perspective, Solomon's temple was a massive
upgrade over the tabernacle. From a divine point of view, the two
worship facilities served the same purpose.

• • •

The Old Testament word for *temple* is often translated "house."
It simply means "a place of habitation." Previously, God had filled
the tabernacle with His glory (Exodus 40:34–35). Once Solomon's temple was completed and dedicated (2 Chronicles 7:1), God
"moved in" there. In effect, the temple was God's earthly house.

Though the Bible teaches that God is everywhere (see Psalm 139; Acts 17:24–28), the Old Testament shows how God localized His presence in a special way at the Jewish temple—specifically in an innermost room called the Holy of Holies (or Most Holy Place).

This is the reason devout Jews pray so reverently at the Western Wall in Jerusalem. It's believed that just beyond that wall is the spot where, in ancient times, God's glory dwelled.

●　●　●

Solomon's great temple was destroyed in 587 BC by the Babylonians (2 Kings 25:8–17). But the Bible speaks of other later temples. The Jewish exiles who were allowed to return to Jerusalem from Babylonian captivity, beginning in 537 BC, constructed a second, less impressive temple on the same site (Haggai 2).

Around 20 BC, Herod the Great began a major temple makeover. The result was the temple that Jesus frequented, and that He called "my Father's house" (see John 2:16). Immediately after saying that, He also referred to His own body as a "temple" (vv. 19–22).

In the early church, a new view of the temple began to emerge. Leaders like Stephen and Paul declared matter-of-factly that God doesn't live in man-made structures (Acts 7:44–50; 17:24). Rather, in Paul's words, those with faith in Jesus—individually and corporately—are said to be the temple of God (1 Corinthians 3:16–17; 2 Corinthians 6:16–7:1; Ephesians 2:19–22).

●　●　●

Challenge yourself with these questions: What if Paul's words are true? What if, when a person puts his or her trust in Christ, God Almighty moves into that individual's life—and dwells there forever?

In that case, instead of one fixed house in one location, God has millions of living, breathing houses all over creation.

If that doesn't show us God's desire to live among all people everywhere, it's hard to know what would.

WALK

To move steadily by foot, or figuratively,
to conduct one's self in a certain way

He forsook the LORD, the God of his ancestors, and did not walk in
obedience to him. (2 KINGS 21:22)

If you had nineteen of anything—vacations, jobs, coworkers, apples—wouldn't you expect at least one of them to be good, or at the very least, so-so?

Nobody goes zero for nineteen, right?

Wrong.

From 931 BC (when Israel split into two kingdoms after the death of Solomon) to 722 BC (when the Assyrians invaded), the Northern Kingdom of Israel was ruled by nineteen evil kings in a row. Nineteen!

The Southern Kingdom of Judah fared slightly better—and therefore lasted a little while longer. Out of twenty kings, they had eight who the Bible says "walked" in obedience to God.

By the way, "walking" with God wasn't just a requirement for Israel's leaders. It was a command for all God's people (Deuteronomy 8:6).

• • •

The common Old Testament Hebrew word translated "walk"* means just what we think: to move in a certain direction by

---

*The Hebrew word for *walk* is *halak*.

putting one foot in front of the other. In the Bible, however, "walking" is often figurative. It refers metaphorically to a person's conduct or manner of life. To walk is to behave in a certain way. According to the Bible, it's possible to "walk righteously" (Isaiah 33:15). It's also possible to walk "with falsehood" (Job 31:5) and in "dark ways" (Proverbs 2:13).

• • •

We sometimes say things like, "If you're not careful, you're going to end up where you're headed!" As cheesy as statements like that are, there's a truckload of truth behind them. The fact is, at any given moment, one's life *does* have a trajectory. By the choices we make and the actions we take, we are moving in a certain direction. We're all walking somewhere!

The person who walks with honesty will ultimately gain a reputation for integrity. The person who goes down a path of duplicity will never end up in a place of honor.

This is why the apostle Paul urged in the New Testament, "Be careful how you walk" (Ephesians 5:15 NASB) and "walk in a manner worthy of the Lord" (Colossians 1:10 ESV).

Clearly the walking he was referring to has more to do with our hearts than with our feet.

• • •

Anyone who's ever tried to stumble to the bathroom at night knows how dangerous it can be to walk in darkness. Spiritually speaking, the good news, according to the apostle John, is that ample light is available to believers (1 John 1:6–7). And wrong, dark paths can be abandoned (v. 9).

The gospel means we can learn to walk in new ways (see Romans 6:4).

RECORDS

A list of genealogical data or an
accounting of historical facts

As for the events of King David's reign, from beginning to end, they
are written in the records of Samuel the seer, the records of Nathan the
prophet and the records of Gad the seer. (1 Chronicles 29:29)

Think of all the information the human race currently stores in "the cloud."

Now, imagine where we'd be if "the cloud" suddenly did what regular clouds do—disappeared forever over the horizon. Or consider how we'd manage if "the cloud" suddenly opened up—and rained all its bits and bytes of electronic data on our unsuspecting heads!

The ancient people of God didn't have "the cloud." No supercomputers or servers, no hard drives or terabytes. But that didn't stop them from keeping a host of holy records.

• • •

Two things stand out about 1 Chronicles.

First, it's almost like an ancient spreadsheet of information pertaining to David's reign: genealogical data and detailed lists of all kinds—the names and job titles of various government workers, army divisions, building materials, and key military victories.

At the end of 1 Chronicles, the writer—likely the priest Ezra—mentions other collections of "records" (see 1 Chronicles 29:29 above). Ezra uses the common Hebrew term that is usually translated "word."* In this context, it clearly means something like "a summary of key information" or "the official minutes."

The second thing Bible readers encounter when they read 1 Chronicles is a déjà vu feeling: *Wait a minute . . . didn't I already read all this stuff about David?*

And the answer is "Yes. You did." The books of 1 and 2 Samuel give a historical and political snapshot of the lives and reigns of Saul and David, Israel's first two kings. The books of 1 and 2 Chronicles offer a spiritual summary of David's dynasty. Whereas 1 and 2 Samuel focus on the flaws of Israel's kings, 1 and 2 Chronicles emphasize the faithfulness of Israel's God—and show that He keeps tabs on His people.

● ● ●

In a broad sense, if we believe the assorted documents we call the Bible are divinely inspired (see chapter 88), then the inclusion of books like 1 Chronicles reveals an overlooked truth: *God keeps records.*

● ● ●

We tend to think only certain people and tasks are important. The books of Chronicles—like the credits at the end of a movie— show that God sees and takes note of everything and everybody.

Lahmi (1 Chronicles 20:5), the big guy who opposed God's people—God knows what he did. The talented singer

---

*The Hebrew word is *dabar.*

Jerimoth (1 Chronicles 25:4)—he's not a household name down here. However, his contribution is well known in heaven.

Today when you see any sort of list (or when someone mentions "the cloud"), remember the surprising truth revealed by 1 Chronicles: God keeps records!

EXILE

To be forced to leave one's home

[Nebuchadnezzar] carried into exile to Babylon the remnant,
who escaped from the sword, and they became servants to him
and his successors until the kingdom of Persia came to power.

(2 Chronicles 36:20)

We put misbehaving toddlers in "time out." Disruptive students get sent to detention. Common criminals get cuffed and carted off by courageous cops (try saying that ten times quickly).

And when God's ancient people continually broke the covenant promises they'd freely made to Him, how did He respond?

He sent them into exile.

• • •

The Hebrew verb translated "exile" means "to uncover or remove."* In other contexts—like the one above—it means "to remove *by taking captive*." It's the idea of deporting or expelling people from their country.

---

* *Galah* is the Hebrew word translated "exile."

The Old Testament includes a story in which God told the prophet Ezekiel to pack his bags and make a big public show of leaving his house, digging a hole in the wall of Jerusalem (see Ezekiel 12:1–11), and departing the city through it. The divine message via this odd, nonverbal sermon? *This is what will happen to you if you don't turn back to me. You'll be forced to leave your homes and live elsewhere.*

Sure enough, when the people of the Northern Kingdom of Israel disregarded the warnings of multiple prophets, they were overrun by the Assyrians in 722 BC. Ripped from their homeland, they were forced to relocate to Assyria (2 Kings 15:29; 17:6).

Sadly, the residents of the Southern Kingdom of Judah also experienced the pain of exile. After continually straying from God, they were uprooted from Judah and Jerusalem by the Babylonians and taken into captivity beginning in 605 BC.

• • •

In truth, exile is a recurring theme in the Bible. Adam and Eve (and all their descendants) were "banished" from Eden following their sin (Genesis 3:23–24). After cheating his brother, Esau, Jacob had no choice but to leave his home (Genesis 27:41–45). Joseph, through no fault of his own (other than maybe being a little cocky), ended up in a foreign place after his brothers sold him into slavery (Genesis 37:12–36). David, after being anointed as Israel's next king (1 Samuel 16:13), spent years in a kind of "mobile exile"—constantly on the run, trying to stay one step ahead of the paranoid King Saul.

Spiritually speaking, the Bible says we're all exiles. We were designed to live in a perfect world—in face-to-face intimacy with God (Genesis 1–2). The consequences of our sin ripped us away from all that.

• • •

In Acts 7, when Stephen was reciting a quick history of the Jewish people, he talked about their exile using a Greek verb that literally means "to change one's home."*

In the best sense of the word, this is what the gospel does: It gives us a new home. When we believe in Jesus, we're no longer citizens of earth. We become members of God's forever kingdom.

So, if in this world, we sometimes feel homesick or out of place, like we're aliens or exiles (see 1 Peter 2:11), it's because we are.

But not forever.

---

*Stephen employed a form of the Greek verb *metoikizo*.

REMNANT

That which is left—especially after a calamity

But now we have been given a brief moment of grace,
for the LORD our God has allowed a few of us to survive as a remnant.
(EZRA 9:8 NLT)

Have you noticed how the Bible continually makes a big deal about small things?

It tells the larger-than-life story of how a tiny family ended up blessing the whole world. It tells smaller stories within that story: about a ragtag army of 300 defeating a much larger foe (Judges 7), a shepherd boy cutting a giant down to size (1 Samuel 17), and a little kid's lunch feeding an enormous crowd (John 6:9–14). In the book of God, we read about how a tiny speck of faith can move mountains (Luke 17:6) and how a small bit of false teaching can cause widespread damage (Galatians 5:7–9).

The Bible highlights little things that the world usually overlooks. Which is why the Bible also talks about remnants.

• • •

The Hebrew word translated "remnant" sometimes means "the state of being out of captivity or danger." Here the idea is "the remainder, the leftover part that survives."

After the Persian king Cyrus conquered Babylonia, he gave the Jews exiled there permission to go back to Judah and rebuild their decimated country. Only a small number of Jews—a remnant—elected to return to Jerusalem. The majority stayed in Mesopotamia—or relocated to other areas in the ancient world.

The book of Ezra documents how these returning Jews arrived in two groups. The first, some 50,000 people under the leadership of Zerubbabel, a devout public official, came to rebuild the Jewish temple (Ezra 1–6). A few decades later, a second group—about 1,750 people—returned with Ezra the priest to shore up the hearts of the discouraged remnant (Ezra 7–10).

● ● ●

Worldly wisdom says that bigger is better, and most is best. So given the choice—would you rather be part of the majority or the minority?—most people don't even hesitate. "Be part of a *remnant*? Uh, no thanks."

And yet it's worth repeating again: The Bible makes much of the few, and is unimpressed by the crowd. Only two of the twelve spies sent to do reconnaissance in the promised land came back with a God-honoring "let's go!" recommendation (Numbers 13–14). Only a few people in the first century church at Sardis were commended by the Lord—the rest were rebuked (Revelation 3:1–6). Only a few people, according to Jesus, ever find the road "that leads to life" (Matthew 7:14).

● ● ●

Being part of a remnant usually means funny looks, whispers, shaking heads—or worse. So be it.

The Bible makes it clear that where we stand—and with whom—matters far more than how many happen to be standing with us.

AWESOME

Expressive of a divine quality or act that inspires
deep reverence of holy fear

Don't be afraid of them. Remember the Lord, who is great and awesome.

(NEHEMIAH 4:14)

According to the Bible, God is awesome.

According to multiple film critics, so is the latest superhero movie. Your best friend insists your tan is awesome (which is also the word she keeps using to describe the dress she bought last week—and the new smartphone app she's been using to sell neighbors all the junk that no longer fits in her basement).

Think the awesomeness stops there? Not even close. People on social media are raving about how awesome your vacation pictures look. And, shock of all shocks: last night your picky, fast-food-loving nine-year-old deemed grilled veggies *awesome*.

Maybe the catchy song from the awesome kids' movie got it right after all—maybe "everything *is* awesome"?

Or maybe not.

• • •

The Hebrew words translated "awesome" in the Old Testament all convey the idea of reverential fear. This isn't fear as in "receiving a mild scare." This is fear as in "being steamrolled by holy dread." This kind of awesome needs a defibrillator. It leaves a person breathless, unable to move or speak or put coherent thoughts together.

The roughly thirty occurrences of the word *awesome* in the Bible all revolve around God—people coming undone because of His glorious presence, folks stunned into silence or reduced to tears by His unimaginable plans and towering works.

• • •

That new best-selling novel on your nightstand might be thrilling, and your friend's new house might be lovely, but awesome? *Awesome* is the reason people fall instinctively to their knees when they encounter God. His shattering holiness makes prophets shake and shiver (Isaiah 6:1–5). His astonishing power makes apostles want to run for their lives (Luke 5:8–9)! His unfathomable wisdom leaves even the most devout saints speechless (Job 40:3–5).

And that's only scratching the surface of True Awesome. Let's not forget God's never-ending love, His compassion for the forgotten and broken, and the gracious, glorious claim of the gospel, that "while we were still sinners, Christ died for us" (Romans 5:8).

• • •

Let's make this personal. Does the reality of God ever stop you in your tracks? Does the love of Jesus—at least sometimes—cause you to shake your head in wide-eyed astonishment?

Ask the only One truly worthy of the description "awesome" to help you recover this kind of stunned wonder. Ask Him to awe you in fresh ways today.

ENEMIES

Those who are hostile to God, His plans, or His people

> He told them to celebrate these days with feasting and gladness and by giving
> gifts of food to each other and presents to the poor. This would commemorate
> a time when the Jews gained relief from their enemies, when their sorrow was
> turned into gladness and their mourning into joy. (ESTHER 9:22 NLT)

Tucked away in the Old Testament is a story as riveting as any suspense thriller you'll ever read. The book of Esther focuses on the Jews who elected to remain in Persia even after King Darius gave them permission to return to their homeland.

The story has a little bit of everything—a drunken feast and an outsized harem, an assassination plot and a genocidal villain—with an execution thrown in for good measure. All this takes place in a setting that swirls with prejudice, suspicion, and lust. No joke—the book of Esther is a page-turner, with enough plot twists to give you whiplash.

Oddly, the story never mentions God. Instead, it slyly shows His providential, behind-the-scenes care for His people. And it echoes an unsettling truth that the Bible declares from Genesis to Revelation:

Some people are sworn enemies of God and His people.

• • •

The common word translated "enemy" almost three hundred times in the Old Testament means "a hostile foe."* In this case, the powerful foe of the Jews in Persia during the time of Esther was Haman, a high-ranking government official. When he felt disrespected by Mordecai, one of the Jewish exiles, the enraged Haman set into motion a plot to exterminate the Jewish race.

What Haman didn't know is that God had already promised His people, "I will be an enemy to your enemies" (Exodus 23:22). Lest we reveal too many spoilers here, let's just say, Haman's plans ran into some considerable snags. When all was said and done, the Jews ended up with an annual spring holiday (still celebrated today) that involves lots of eating and drinking and crazy fun.

● ● ●

Haman is only one in a revolving door of enemies that have threatened God's people throughout history: The Egyptians. All those "ites" (Amalekites and Midianites and Moabites and Canaanites and Amorites and Ammonites and Hittites and Edomites). The Philistines. The Syrians. The Assyrians. The Babylonians. The Greeks. The Romans. (And that list only gets us to the first century!)

What the Bible says and what history shows is that if you oppose God or His people, it won't be pretty.

● ● ●

The New Testament begins with a Jew named Jesus coming on the scene, making messianic claims, making disciples, and making countless enemies! Before His death, Christ warned His followers to expect the same kind of hostility (John 15:18). And yet Jesus said, don't try to get back at your enemies (Matthew 5:38–39).

---

* *Enemies* is the plural form of the Hebrew *'oyeb.*

That's God's job (Romans 12:17–21). Instead, He insisted, love them (Matthew 5:44).

What specifically would that look like in your life today?

SATAN

The powerful enemy of God who opposes
His plan and His people

The LORD said to Satan, "Where have you come from?"
Satan answered the LORD, "From roaming throughout the earth,
going back and forth on it." (JOB 1:7)

Every great story has an antagonist: an opponent of the main character.

In the great story of God, that villain is Satan. (Like most antagonists, he has a host of aliases: the devil, the serpent, the dragon, Lucifer, Beelzebul, and Belial.*)

The name *Satan* appears for the first time in 1 Chronicles 21—where he was blamed for inciting David to count his troops rather than trust his God. In the book of Job, Satan's character is revealed more fully. With the angels, he appears before God. When God starts bragging about "my servant Job," Satan scoffs that Job's "upright" character is only because he's been so "blessed" (Job 1:8–10). Allow some tragedy in his life, the enemy hisses to God, and Job will "surely curse you to your face" (v. 11).

And thus begins the weirdest wager ever.

• • •

---

*See Matthew 4:1; Genesis 3:1; Revelation 20:2; Isaiah 14:12; Matthew 12:24; and 2 Corinthians 6:15.

The name *Satan* is straight from the Hebrew. It means "adversary." And does the description ever fit! In other places in the Bible, Satan is labeled "the prince of demons" (Matthew 12:24), "the god of this age" (2 Corinthians 4:4), "the ruler of the kingdom of the air" (Ephesians 2:2)—even "a roaring lion looking for someone to devour" (1 Peter 5:8).

As to the question of where such an evil creature came from, the majority view of Bible scholars and preachers is that Satan was originally an angel himself—perhaps the first and most glorious of the angels. Then, in a prideful attempt to take the place of God, he "broke bad," convincing a third of the angels in heaven to join in his futile rebellion.*

• • •

Jesus regarded Satan as real, not the personification of evil in the world, but as an actual spiritual being. The Bible declares the devil dangerous—and says we should watch vigilantly for his schemes (Ephesians 6:11).

Yet the clear testimony of Scripture is that even though the enemy of our souls is powerful, he's no match for God. In Jesus's sinless life, sacrificial death, and glorious resurrection, Satan has been defeated. His demonic plans have been ruined (1 John 3:8). The devil knows he's going down in flames (literally, see Revelation 20:10). Now, like a suicide bomber or kamikaze pilot, he's trying to take as many people with him as he can.

• • •

We need to guard against the extremes of either dismissing talk of "the devil" as superstitious nonsense or imagining there are demons lurking around every corner.

---

*This interpretation comes from a correlation of assorted Bible passages: Isaiah 14:12–14; Ezekiel 28:14; Matthew 4:8–9; John 8:44; 1 John 3:8; Revelation 12:7–9.

The twofold message of the Bible to believers? (1) You have a fierce enemy, so be careful. (2) You have an awesome Savior, so be confident.

ANSWER

To say something in reply

I spoke once, but I have no answer—twice, but I will say no more.

(JOB 40:5)

You don't have to be a Mensa member to see why we're so ob-sessed with answers. It's because life constantly confronts us with questions.

Chief among them: If God is all-loving and all-powerful, why does He permit evil? Why do innocent people suffer? And why do bad people get to laugh their way to the bank (or to the beach, or to some other kind of blessing)?

It's fitting that one of the oldest writings in the Bible—the book of Job—touches on these issues. In Job we meet the kind of man we'd want for a father, a friend, or a boss. He's God-fearing. He's got integrity in spades.

But then Satan (see chapter 29) gets permission to turn Job's life into a living hell. In one terrible day Job loses all *ten* of his children, plus all his lesser wealth. Soon after that, the devil takes away Job's health.

As you'd imagine, it isn't long before the questions are fly-ing—as well as the demands for answers.

• • •

Found more than twenty times in the book of Job, the Hebrew verb translated "answer" means "to give a response."* It conveys the idea of making your case, explaining yourself, spelling out the reasons for your actions or predicament.

When Job's friends first arrive, they resist asking questions or offering answers. In truth, they are model counselors. They sit quietly, weeping with their shattered friend. But when the grieving Job starts in with all his *whys*, the friends unload.

For thirty-four chapters, Job and these armchair theologians fire questions back and forth at each another, and attempt to offer reasons—answers—for Job's calamity.

In the end, God finally joins the conversation. He answers Job from out of a storm (Job 38:1). But He doesn't specifically address any of Job's questions. Instead, He rattles off fifty or so questions for Job (see 38:2–41:34) and tells the others their answers are all wrong (42:7–10).

● ● ●

Job—and the psalmists too—show that it's okay to bring our questions to God (where else would we take them?). But their experience also demonstrates that God doesn't feel the need to explain himself. Rather than provide us answers, He brings us himself. But, of course! While logical explanations can address the questions in our heads, they can never soothe the pain in our hearts.

● ● ●

Two things are true when we face heartache: (1) It is normal to ask "Why?" and (2) it is wise to remember that this side of heaven, we're not likely to get the answers we seek. In the end, the best we can do is surrender our situations to God.

And when we have friends in pain, let's learn from Job's answer-gushing friends: love, don't lecture.

---

*For those who care about such things, the Hebrew word is *anah*.

PSALM

A prayer or spiritual expression set to music

A psalm of David. When he fled from his son Absalom. (Psalm 3 title)

The book at the heart of the Bible—literally and, many would argue figuratively—is Psalms. In an unfiltered, almost shocking way, this collection of writings describes the ups and downs of real people trying to live by faith.

In some, the author is close to waving the white flag. Here he's describing the heaviness of guilt. There it's the double whammy of being terrified by some looming disaster *and* mystified that God doesn't seem to care. As we read, we don't even notice that we're slowing down, gawking, rubbernecking. Who can't relate to such feelings?

In other spots the writer's joy dazzles like the rising sun. These readings are painful to read in a whole different way. We think, *Have I ever been that alive?* But again, we can't seem to turn away. So we squint, hoping to soak in a smidgen of all that glory. One day, perhaps we will come to love and trust God like that.

Those who read the Psalms—and who are honest—tend to agree: as a group, these writings are marked by the same sort of "spiritual schizophrenia" that grips most of us most days, as we careen wildly between belief and doubt.

• • •

Our English word *psalm* is a translation of a Hebrew noun that means "song or melody."*

Basically then, a psalm is a prayer (or declaration about God) meant for singing. The Bible includes 150 of these ancient compositions, making the book of Psalms, at least in English, the longest book in the Bible.† Together these laments, praises, and songs of trust make up the worship manual of ancient Israel. They're the "hymnal," so to speak, that Jesus would have used. About half the collection is attributed to David, explaining how he got the title, "the sweet psalmist of Israel" (2 Samuel 23:1 NLT, NASB, ESV).

It's interesting that even though the Psalms were originally meant to be sung, nobody preserved a single chord chart. We don't have a clue what the original tunes might have sounded like. Even so, the Psalms remain the ultimate collection of "oldies but goodies." People can't get enough of them! Bible Gateway, a popular searchable online Bible, reports that its users read the Psalms more than they read any other book of Scripture.

● ● ●

Whatever the state of your soul (hopeless or hopeful, discouraged or delighted), whatever your need (rescue, a quick reminder of what's true, a reason to rejoice, or just hearing another struggling saint say a version of "Me too"), the Psalms have got you covered.

"You're not alone," these ancient songs sing softly. "Others have been where you are. And behind all your mess—and through all your struggles—stands One who will never abandon you. He's big. He's good. He alone is worthy of your attention and affection. By faith, praise Him!"

---

* *Psalm* is *mizmor* in Hebrew. It comes from the verb *zamar*, which means "to sing praise or make music."

† Bible scholars note that when we compare the books of the Bible in their original languages, Jeremiah is the longest, followed by Genesis. Psalms is third.

• • •

It's said that the late great Billy Graham made it his practice to read five psalms every day—in order to make his way through this rich old songbook each month. As spiritual habits go, you would be hard-pressed to develop one more useful than that.

KEEP

To watch over carefully; to guard and care for

The LORD will protect you from all evil; He will keep your soul.
(PSALM 121:7 NASB)

W e're surrounded by an array of keepers—bookkeepers and housekeepers, barkeepers and innkeepers, gatekeepers and groundskeepers. Live long enough, and chances are good you'll meet a goalkeeper, maybe even a beekeeper. But beyond all the storekeepers and doorkeepers, there's one Keeper to beat them all.

• • •

In Psalm 121, an unnamed psalmist—who makes it clear from the start that he is desperate for some help—speaks of God as the keeper of His people. Not once or twice, but *six* times in eight verses he uses the Hebrew verb translated "keep."*

For anyone in trouble—which is some of us all the time, and all of us some of the time—this lovely word is a lifeline. *Keep* conveys the idea of watching carefully and guarding vigilantly. The verb also suggests caring for or tending to whatever it is that one is keeping.

---

*The word is *shamar.*

God—the psalmist is saying—is like that perfectionistic timekeeper who monitors the clock obsessively, down to the millisecond. The Almighty is like that no-nonsense record keeper who meticulously remembers where every box and file is, and who can tell you exactly what is in them all. God's like that devoted zookeeper who notices the one sloth that is a moving a tad slower than the rest of its lethargic kin—and who drops everything to find out why.

● ● ●

Keeping isn't just the obsession of one frantic psalmist. This idea permeates the Bible. Forms of the word are found more than 460 times! Not all of these references point to God. In fact, the very first occurrence of the word is in the opening paragraphs of Scripture when God puts Adam in the garden to work it and "take care of it" (Genesis 2:15). The word is also used in the sense of God's people being vigilant to carry out God's commands, like when Moses told the Israelites, "you must be *careful* to obey all the decrees and regulations I am giving you today" (Deuteronomy 11:32 NLT emphasis added).

● ● ●

Whatever you've been tasked with keeping today—the minutes of the meeting, a secret, your best friend's kids—know this: God is keeping *you*. That fact alone is enough to give you the strength to be your brother's keeper or a peacekeeper. It's enough to keep you *from* keeping score, which inevitably leads to keeping grudges.

Bottom line, we are kept. That, my friend, is what keeps us going.

HEART

The immaterial control center of a person's life—
where we feel, think, and decide

My heart has heard you say, "Come and talk with me." And my heart responds,
"LORD, I am coming." (PSALM 27:8 NLT)

I t isn't just contemporary culture that talks (and sings) exten-
sively about the heart—for example, about people being big-
hearted, or heartless, or brokenhearted. The word *heart* is front
and center throughout the Bible—occurring some 900 times!
    Why is this word so prominent in Scripture?

• • •

Biblical references to the heart seldom have to do with the
blood-pumping organ in the human chest.* In fact, the great majority of mentions refer to the immaterial part of the human personality—what many call the spirit, soul, or invisible self. Simply
put, the heart is the control center of a person's life.
    Western culture tends to restrict the heart to the "touchy-
feely" part of the human personality. The Bible, however, speaks

---

*The Old Testament Hebrew word for *heart* is *leb*. The New Testament Greek equivalent is
kardia—from which we get our English word *cardiology*.

of the heart as the place where we feel *and* think *and* decide. In other words, the sharp distinction that we moderns make between the heart and mind isn't found in Scripture. God's Word uses the words interchangeably.

In the Psalms, the heart is said to be where—among many other things—we meditate (4:4), feel glad (4:7) give thanks (9:1), rejoice (19:8), and trust (28:7). It's where we entertain sinful urges (36:1) or God-honoring desires (37:4). It's where we imagine (73:7), feel wounded (109:22) or dismayed (143:4), test God (78:18), and seek God (119:10).

● ● ●

A major principle of Scripture is that the condition of our hearts determines the direction of our lives (see Proverbs 4:23). If we have humble (Psalm 131:1), undivided (86:11), steadfast (112:7) hearts, if our hearts are marked by purity (24:4), integrity (101:2), sorrow over sin (51:17), and wisdom (90:12), we will live in ways that honor God and encourage others.

On the other hand, if our hearts are infected with pride (131:1), stubbornness (81:12), or perversity (101:4), our actions will display those qualities.

● ● ●

When certain symptoms arise—an irregular heartbeat, chest pain, dizziness—wise people don't play around. They make their way to the nearest emergency room.

In the same way, when we start noticing warning signs in our character—bad attitudes, foul language, or selfish actions— we have to act quickly. Something's wrong with our heart! Wise believers make a beeline for the one the Bible calls the knower of hearts (see Acts 1:24). He alone is able to diagnose the problem (Psalm 139:23) and put us back on a path to spiritual health.

HALLELUJAH

An expression of praise or an exhortation to gush over God

Praise the LORD. Give thanks to the LORD, for he is good;
his love endures forever. (PSALM 106:1)

Not everyone realizes that multiple words in our English vernacular come straight from the Hebrew. We're talking wonderful words like *cherub, sabbatical, rabbi, schmooze, Messiah, kosher, jubilee, behemoth, satanic,* and *amen*—plus all sorts of popular personal names like *Abigail, Samuel, Abraham, Sarah, David, Joshua, Rebekah, Benjamin, Jacob, Jonathan,* and more.

Such lexical riches are enough to make a person say, "Hallelujah!"

• • •

Oh, yes—*hallelujah*! How could we forget *that* beautiful Hebrew word? It comes from two words—*hallel,* meaning "to praise," and *yah,* a shortened form of *Yahweh,* the covenant name of Israel's God. In the Old Testament, *hallelujah* is found only in the book of Psalms—north of twenty times—but most English Bibles translate it "praise the LORD."

In the New Testament the expression occurs four times, all in the book of Revelation. There, even though the apostle John is writing in Greek, he doesn't bother translating the word from Hebrew. "Hallelujah!" he describes the throngs in heaven shouting in unison. And the effect, he says, is like a roaring river or waterfall, deafening like thunder (Revelation 19:1–6).

• • •

Lots of people ask why it's good—and even "fitting" (Psalm 33:1)—to live a hallelujah lifestyle. Think about it this way:

Let's say you're privileged to witness something truly spectacular: a bona fide medical miracle, a natural wonder like the Northern Lights, an athletic performance for the ages, or an iconic musical or theatrical event. Now, imagine not being allowed to express any sort of response. You have to remain calm and keep your lips buttoned. You're forbidden to "ooh and ah" or even whisper "wow!" You're certainly not allowed to cheer, clap, brag on the exploits of the artist, or chant the name of the performer.

Talk about frustrating! In fact, not being allowed to express admiration or awe would almost ruin the experience! C. S. Lewis explained why, noting that true praise is never an obligation—it's always a delight! Praise is our natural, unforced response to greatness and beauty. And, actually, when we *don't* gush over praiseworthy people and laudable things, we experience far less joy!

• • •

From start to finish, the Bible not only makes much of God, it encourages its readers to do likewise. We're to give thinks (Psalm 107) in all things (1 Thessalonians 5:18). We're to find joy in focusing on who God is and all He has done to rescue and redeem us.

Ask God to help you cultivate a heart that sees the majesty of God all around you and that routinely speaks a little Hebrew, specifically . . .

"Hallelujah!"

SELAH

A reminder to pause and reflect on lofty eternal truths

I stretch out my hands to You; My soul longs for You,
as a parched land. Selah. (PSALM 143:6 NASB)

To all the folks who are constantly blowing and going, moving and shaking, wheeling and dealing...

And to all the other weary souls who are running around like the proverbial chicken with its head cut off, thereby meeting themselves coming and going, and barely staying ahead of the train...

Here's a timely Bible word for you from the book of Psalms: *Selah.*

• • •

The mysterious Hebrew word *selah* is found seventy-one times in the Psalms (and three more places in Habakkuk). Scholars are divided as to what exactly the word means—though there's no shortage of ideas.

We know that *selah* is related to a verb that means "to lift up." So, for example, Moses referenced the way the Egyptian pharaoh *exalted himself* against the Israelites (Exodus 9:17). And the prophets used the metaphor of a road being *built up* (that is, an elevated "highway," see Isaiah 57:14 and Jeremiah 18:15). Another form of this verb is translated "ladder" or "stairway" in Genesis 28:12.

In the Psalms, *selah* is often inserted at section or stanza breaks or at the end of lines, for example, "The LORD of hosts is with us; the God of Jacob is our stronghold. Selah" (Psalm 46:7 NASB).

Because of all these factors, many theorize that *selah* was a worship notation for the ancient Israelites. Perhaps the idea was "Lift up your voice" or "Let the music swell." Others believe *selah* was a call for some kind of musical "interlude" (that's how several English translations render it). And if so, while the music continued, worshipers were expected to pause and reflect on the lofty lyrics just sung—to focus on higher realities and let their hearts rejoice in eternal truths.

• • •

We live in a world that worships at the altars of hurry, efficiency, and productivity. You've heard the mantras: Get more done in less time! Don't stop—you'll fall behind! He who hesitates is lost!

Without realizing it, this same kind of frenetic mind-set can mar our efforts to connect with God. Reading the Bible becomes an item to cross off on the old to-do list. Prayer ends up being little more than a spiritual speed bump. Corporate worship services are crammed so full there's no opportunity for reflection or quiet contemplation.

In other words, no *selah*!

• • •

How about we bring *selah* back into vogue? And not just the word, but the actual practice.

What if every time we read, heard, or remembered an eternal truth—or saw the grace of God displayed powerfully in someone's life—what if, instead of nodding mindlessly and turning to the next item on the agenda, we said, "Selah."

What if we paused, lifted our eyes to heaven, and maybe our voices in praise?

What if, indeed.

PROVERB

A concise, memorable saying intended
to impart wise counsel

The proverbs of Solomon the son of David, king of Israel.

(PROVERBS 1:1)

Every culture collects proverbs, and it's not hard to see why. Good proverbs are what Twitter wants to be, but rarely is: pithy and profound. Good proverbs make us think and smile or even wince. They offer wise reminders and much-needed correction. For example:

"The person who gossips *with* you will gossip *about* you."
—Irish proverb

"Never write a letter* when you're angry." —Chinese proverb

"Give a man a fish, and he eats for a day. Teach a man to fish, and you'll never see him again." —American proverb

The ancient Hebrews collected proverbs too. It helped that they had a wise king—Solomon—who flung good proverbs around the way some people toss confetti on New Year's Eve.

---

*We could add "or a text or an email or a social media post."

According to Bible Gateway, the previously mentioned online Bible, the book of Proverbs—attributed mostly to King Solomon—is the fifth most popular of the Bible's sixty-six books.

• • •

The Hebrew word for "proverb" is related to a verb that means "to be comparable to."* A proverb then is a short saying that compares two things. It's a form of wisdom literature that functions like a mini-parable. Someone makes a perceptive observation about life, and then expresses it in a clear and memorable way.

A classic example is Proverbs 12:18: "The words of the reckless pierce like swords, but the tongue of the wise brings healing."

Brilliant! In one sentence we get a vivid, memorable, eye-opening comparison between the damaging effects of careless speech and the healing impact of wise expression.

• • •

Who among us doesn't need practical wisdom—every day of our lives? Could you use insights about work or parenting or resolving conflict? How about admonitions to associate with the honorable people and warnings against running off at the mouth or trusting in your wealth? Need some encouragements to live with integrity or reminders about what happens to those who live with no thought of God? The proverbs in the ancient book of Proverbs offer these kinds of insights and more.

It's crucial to remember that proverbs are not promises. Unless they specifically mention God's character or conduct, we shouldn't see them as iron-clad guarantees, but rather as general observations about life in a fallen world.

---

* *Proverb* is *mashal* in Hebrew. That fact and a couple bucks will get you a small coffee most places.

• • •

Are Solomon's wise words really worth our time and attention—especially when we could be binge-watching that new reality TV show everyone's raving about?

Depends on if we believe this proverb: "Walk with the wise and become wise, for a companion of fools suffers harm" (Proverbs 13:20).

WISDOM

Skill in living; intelligence of the heart

Get wisdom, get understanding; do not forget my words
or turn away from them. (PROVERBS 4:5)

Everywhere we look, we see smart people: The eighth-grader across town who just made a perfect 1600 on the SAT. The neighbor who's fluent in five languages (and is now in Asia learning a sixth). The professor at the nearby university who was recently nominated for a Nobel Prize in astrophysics.

When surrounded by geniuses and prodigies, it's easy to feel like a dunce. However, the Bible makes it clear that intellect isn't everything, and having a high IQ won't solve all our problems. According to the Good Book, what we need far more than intelligence is wisdom.

• • •

In Hebrew, *wisdom* is *hokmah* (a fun word to say because it sounds like you have a hairball stuck in your throat). In Exodus 28:3, it's used in reference to people with great technical skill and artistic ability.

We could think of *hokmah* as spiritual/moral/relational intelligence. Wise people may not know how to build an app or solve a page of geometry problems, but they have great ingenuity when it comes to navigating life's challenges. They're good at defusing tense situations. They understand and practice the genius of delayed gratification. Because they're humble, they tend to enjoy good relationships.

• • •

Smart people like to debate the notion of whether a person's intelligence is fixed at birth. But whatever we decide about that question, this much is true: we can always increase in wisdom. (How else can we interpret Solomon's counsel to his sons, and to us, to "Get wisdom"?)

And, boy (or girl), do we ever need to get wiser! Because, clearly, knowledge alone won't cut it. Some of the smartest people in the world—people with advanced degrees and brilliant minds and knowledge out the wazoo—keep making giant messes out of their lives, relationships, and reputations. Turns out brainiacs *can* often be maniacs.

• • •

If you've got the smarts of an Einstein or a Stephen Hawking, wonderful! Use all that cerebral firepower for the glory of God and the good of the world. But don't stop there. "Get wisdom."

How? Solomon prayed for it (1 Kings 3:4–15). Later, he said wisdom begins to live in us when we fear the Lord (Proverbs 9:10), that is, when we reverently view God as the ultimate source of all wisdom. When we believe that, we start digging into God's Word, and we get wiser still.

Also, hanging around wise people makes us wiser. (Remember: some of the wisest people on earth don't have a high school diploma, much less a college degree.) When you meet a wise soul, stop, look, and listen. Watch what he does. Pay attention to what she says. Ask a million questions. Take copious notes.

FOOL

A person who is spiritually hard-hearted

The wise are cautious and avoid danger; fools plunge ahead
with reckless confidence. (PROVERBS 14:16 NLT)

In our previous stop on this quick tour of priceless Bible words,
we looked at the beauty of wisdom. We said that wisdom is the
ability to meet the pressures and problems of life with great skill.
Wise people aren't just book-smart—they're people-smart,
they're sharp and savvy in all sorts of scenarios. The truly wise are
maestros at dealing with tense disputes, at responding to criticism, at dealing with finances. Sadly, this kind of wisdom isn't a
common commodity.

The truth is that many people wouldn't recognize a wise response if it jumped up and kissed them on the mouth. Give them
a hundred interactions or decisions in a row, and they might very
well make a mess of *every single one.*

The Bible has a word for people with the stunning propensity
to do the wrong thing time after time after time.

That word is *fool.*

• • •

Several different words in Scripture get translated "fool." *Kesil*
is the one that's used most often in the Old Testament poetry
books of Psalms, Proverbs, and Ecclesiastes. *Kesil* conveys the

idea of being morally stubborn or spiritually dull. In other words, being a fool doesn't mean being thick-headed; it means being hard-hearted!

The book of Proverbs is blunt, even brutal, in describing fools. They're the polar opposites of the wise. They're lazy (13:4) and gullible (14:15). They're combative (29:8) and proud (21:24). They don't learn from their mistakes (26:11). And perhaps the biggest knock against fools? They despise and reject any kind of counsel, correction, or advice (1:7; 14:33; 17:10; 23:9).

• • •

It's fashionable now to talk about the "optics" of a situation. This has to do with how certain things look. Guess what? The optics of foolishness are the worst optics imaginable. Who wants to be known as the big mouth, the hothead, the sucker, the person who pushed past all the warning signs and barricades and drove his or her life straight over a cliff?

Proverbs speaks candidly about the future of a fool. Such a person lives with constant conflict and stress (18:6). She brings grief to her family (17:21). He ruins his life (10:8).

• • •

Reading the Bible is like looking in a spiritual mirror. In other words, it shows us the truth about our hearts. If you read Proverbs—and please, by all means, read Proverbs!—you're guaranteed to see yourself in some of its not-so-flattering verses. That's because we all have some foolishness in us. And learning wisdom is a lifelong course.

Don't be discouraged. With God's help you can get there. The goal is to live in such a way that foolishness is more and more descriptive of your past—and wisdom is more descriptive of your present and your future.

39

MEANINGLESS

Vain or fleeting, worthless

"Meaningless! Meaningless!" says the Teacher. "Utterly meaningless! Everything is meaningless." (ECCLESIASTES 1:2)

People who complain that the Bible is uninteresting and irrelevant are like the guy who stares at Michelangelo's *David* and grumbles, "I don't see what all the fuss is about—it's just a big hunk of marble." (For the record, these kinds of statements say more about the one commenting than they do about the thing being discussed.)

Before you dismiss the Bible in such a superficial and cavalier way, you should take a few minutes to read the book of Ecclesiastes. It will change your mind because it is *something else*. Many scholars attribute this ancient writing to Solomon and speculate that he composed it late in his life.

In brief, Ecclesiastes reads like the journal of a depressed billionaire in full midlife crisis mode. Solomon talks candidly about using his vast wealth and power in a no-holds-barred search for happiness and meaning.

"Work, wealth, wine, women—I tried it all," Solomon basically confesses. "Nothing worked. Everything about my life 'under the sun'* felt meaningless."

---

*Solomon used this interesting phrase "under the sun" almost thirty times in Ecclesiastes.

• • •

The Hebrew word translated "meaningless" here is *hebel* (don't worry—that will not be on the test). It's rendered as "worthless" or "vanity" in other Bible versions. Interestingly, about half of the seventy or so uses of this word in the Old Testament are found in the book of Ecclesiastes.

Hebel literally means "breath" or "wind." Something that's *hebel* is here—then, *poof*, it's gone, like vapor. The thought is that there's nothing substantive or enduring about it. To put too much stock or hope in such a fleeting thing is vain at best—insane at worst.

• • •

Who among us can't relate—at multiple points in life—to Solomon's bitter disappointment? We don't need immense assets or lofty connections to realize the truths he discovered: that the world can give us short-term thrills, but never the kind of joy that remains. Earthly things and pleasures might be able to distract us briefly from our deepest longings; they cannot satisfy them.

• • •

At the end of his unflinching look at life "under the sun," Solomon concludes, "Now all has been heard; here is the conclusion of the matter: Fear God and keep his commandments, for this is the duty of all mankind" (Ecclesiastes 12:13).

This is what C. S. Lewis was getting at when he speculated that the world's inability to give us ultimate joy suggests that we were made for another world.

And this is precisely the message of Ecclesiastes—and of the whole Bible. When we find ourselves dissatisfied by meaningless acquisitions and vain activities—none of which ever come close to filling our empty, aching souls—it's time to look up.

Anyone who says Solomon's admissions here are uninteresting and irrelevant is just not paying attention.

BELOVED

An intimate term for a lover

I belong to my beloved, and his desire is for me. (SONG OF SONGS 7:10)

Ever notice how, at a big family reunion, there's always that one odd relative who raises eyebrows, blood pressures, even the temperature in the room? Maybe it's an aging aunt with no filter. Or that long-lost, enigmatic cousin that everyone keeps glancing at and whispering about, but no one knows how to engage.

The point is this: if the books of a Bible were a family, the Song of Songs would be that family member.

Scholars have never agreed on what to make of this odd, blush-worthy composition. Believed by many to be the work of King Solomon, it only mentions God once (see 8:6 NASB). Other biblical writings don't quote it. Probably because it's a fairly explicit love song between a young shepherdess and the man she calls "my beloved."

• • •

The word that gets translated "beloved" (more than thirty times!) in our English translations of the Song of Songs may be connected to a Hebrew verb that means "to boil" (everyone who has ever been smitten or lovestruck nods and smiles at this).* The word

---

*The Hebrew word for *beloved* is *dowd* or *dod*.

has strong romantic and sexual connotations,[*] meaning "lover" is definitely an acceptable translation.

• • •

Some see the Song of Songs as an actual, historical account of the young Solomon's courtship and marriage to the true love of his life (regarding his many other marriages as mere political arrangements). Those who take this view see the book as a divine endorsement of the purity and beauty of sexual intimacy within marriage.

Others see within this occasionally racy record of young married love an allegory of God's undying love for Israel—similar to the divine passion expressed in the book of Hosea. Beyond that, the Song of Songs is also viewed by many as an illustration of Christ's intense, undying love for the church (see Ephesians 5).

• • •

In the New Testament Gospels, Jesus is referred to as God's beloved Son (Matthew 3:17). In the Epistles, those who have placed faith in Christ are repeatedly called the "beloved of God" (Romans 1:7 NASB).

Not to be irreverent, but the point would seem to be that God is wildly in love with His people. If you belong to Him, it's not a stretch to say that thoughts of you make His heart beat faster. He wants to be with you. He comes looking for you. When you're not there, He misses you something fierce.

Given this kind of divine love, maybe our response to God should be like the attitude of the young woman in Song of Songs: "I found the one my heart loves. I held him and would not let him go" (Song of Songs 3:4).

---

[*] See its use in Proverbs 7:18 and Ezekiel 16:8.

LIGHT

Illumination that pushes back the darkness,
enabling one to see

Come, descendants of Jacob, let us walk in the light of the LORD. (ISAIAH 2:5)

God's first recorded words were, "Let there be light" (Genesis 1:3). The human race has been obsessed with light ever since.

Ancient cultures actually worshiped the sun and bowed to the moon. We moderns settle for buying fancy light fixtures and—if only we could—light sabers. We wait, not so patiently, for red lights to turn green. We seek out sages who can shed light on our confusing dilemmas. We try with all our might to avoid being seen by others in a bad light.

Sometimes when we're surrounded by darkness, all we can see is a scant flicker of light in the distance. (Crazy, isn't it, how even *that* somehow puts everything in a new light?)

Other times, God help us, we actually prefer the dark. Our biggest fear then? That certain secrets of ours might come to light.

• • •

The word *light* in the Old Testament* can refer variously to the sun (Job 37:21), to dawn (Judges 16:2), to the bright light of day (2 Kings 7:9).

---

*Several Hebrew words are translated "light" in the Old Testament, the most common being *'or* or *'owr*.

Often, however, the light spoken of in Scripture is metaphorical not literal. Given that darkness is associated with sin (Proverbs 2:13), suffering (Lamentations 3:1), and death (Psalm 88:5), *light* is often used to symbolize the opposite of darkness: blessing (Isaiah 58:8), truth (John 3:21), wisdom (Proverbs 6:23), and justice (Isaiah 42:1–3).

The Psalms not only label God's Word a *lamp* and a *light* (Psalm 119:105), they call the LORD a *light* (Psalm 27:1)—which makes Jesus's New Testament claim to be "the light of the world" (John 8:12) *really* interesting.

● ● ●

As a prophet, Isaiah had a two-part job description: revealing God's plans for the future and reiterating God's commands for the present.

No calling was ever harder. By shining the spotlight of God's truth into a dark culture, he made most of his neighbors furious. And his predictions of even darker days ahead didn't win him any Facebook friend requests either.

But in his gloomy messages he occasionally flashed some hope, a little light at the end of the proverbial tunnel. He spoke of brighter days ahead, in fact, days of radiance and dazzling glory (Isaiah 9:2; 42:6, 16; 49:6; 58:8; 60:1–3, 19–20).

● ● ●

According to the Bible, all light comes from God. Even better, in multiple places, the Almighty's face is described as shining on those He loves (Numbers 6:25; Psalms 31:16; 67:1; 118:27; 119:135).

Given this, it's not surprising that God's people are urged to shine (Matthew 5:16). As we look to God in the midst of a dark world, we reflect His glory. We get to sparkle like the stars in an inky night sky (Philippians 2:15).

SERVANT

One who carries out the wishes of another

After he has suffered, he will see the light of life and be satisfied;

by his knowledge my righteous servant will justify many,

and he will bear their iniquities. (ISAIAH 53:11)

The idea of people being forced into slavery against their will is appalling. We recoil at the thought.

The idea of people agreeing to be the domestic servants of others—for example, butlers, cooks, maids, housekeepers, valets—is intriguing. How else do we explain the immense popularity of a TV show like *Downton Abbey* (2010–2015)?

• • •

The word *servant* pops up all over the Bible—more than eight hundred times in the Old Testament alone!—and is used variously to describe slaves who were captured and sold (Genesis 39:17), people who hired themselves out to others (Deuteronomy 15:12), or even civic employees in service to the king (1 Samuel 18:5).* Also, those called to carry out God's will are labeled *servants* of the Lord (Exodus 32:13; Deuteronomy 34:5; Judges 2:8).

---

*The Hebrew word for *servant* is *ebed*.

• • •

Isaiah the prophet was chosen to be the Lord's servant—even though he admitted to being "a man of unclean lips" (6:5). God also called the nation of Israel "my servant" (41:8–9)—even as He also revealed that judgment was headed their way due to their refusal to serve Him! Then, in chapters 52 and 53, the inspired Isaiah began describing another future servant. A perfectly obedient, highly exalted servant.

This particular servant would be "despised and rejected, . . . a man of suffering, and familiar with pain" (53:3). He would be "led like a lamb to the slaughter" (53:7). The Lord would "crush him" (53:10) by laying on Him "the iniquity of us all" (53:6). This innocent servant would be "punished by God . . . pierced for our transgressions" in order to bring us peace (53:4–5). He would pour "out his life unto death" (53:12), be buried in a rich man's grave (53:9), but somehow "see the light of life" (53:11).

Care to guess whom the New Testament writers ultimately identified as the obedient servant predicted by Isaiah and the other prophets? (Hint: Check out the One who said, "The Son of Man did not come to be served, but to serve, and to give his life as a ransom for many" [Matthew 20:28].)

• • •

This is the mind-boggling claim of the gospel: God sent Christ as the ultimate Servant so that we too might find ultimate happiness in becoming His servants—and also His children and friends.

Two questions to ponder: (1) Have you trusted Christ to pay your ransom? (2) Is the mind-set of Jesus—"I am among you as one who serves" (Luke 22:27)—your mind-set today?

COVENANT

A solemn agreement between two parties

"The days are coming," declares the LORD, "when I will make a new covenant with the people of Israel and with the people of Judah."

(JEREMIAH 31:31)

Covenants?

Hmm . . . let's see . . . there was that time about five years ago when the family two doors down built that massive chicken coop in their backyard. The fowl smell (heh, heh) and that rooster crowing all hours of the day and night had everybody on the block talking incessantly about the "neighborhood covenant."

Also, at the storybook wedding you attended last year, the priest described marriage as a "holy and lasting covenant" (although now it seems the couple thought he called it "a short-term lease agreement").

Fact is, we don't use the word *covenant* much in daily conversation. The Bible, on the other hand, uses the word frequently.

• • •

The Hebrew word is *berit*. There's no consensus about the etymology of the word, scholars agreeing only that it signifies an "agreement" or "treaty," or "the forming of an alliance." (A synonym for *covenant* is the word *testament*.)

In ancient times, the parties to a covenant called witnesses to watch as they made solemn promises or vows (and sometimes wrote down these agreements). Often covenants were ratified by symbolic ceremonies: offerings (Genesis 15:9–10), the erecting of memorial stones (Genesis 31:44–47), the partaking of a meal together (Luke 22).

In Scripture we see both individuals and nations making covenants. However, it's the covenants God made with humans that drive the plot of the Bible. We find the word *covenant* used explicitly in divine promises made to Noah in Genesis 6–9 (the Noahic covenant), Abraham in Genesis 15 and 17 (the Abrahamic covenant), Moses in Exodus 19–25 (the Mosaic covenant), and David in 2 Samuel 7 (the Davidic covenant).

Even though the word *covenant* isn't found in Genesis 1:26–30 and 2:16–17, most consider those promises given to humanity before sin entered the world as the Edenic covenant. Similarly, you'll hear some refer to God's post-Fall promises in Genesis 3:15–19 as the Adamic covenant, and the renewed pledge of land in Deuteronomy 30:1–10 as the Palestinian covenant.

Late in Old Testament history, Jeremiah prophesied a coming "new covenant" (Jeremiah 31:31). This must have been good news to people who were failing miserably at keeping the old Mosaic covenant!

Jesus later claimed this new covenant would come about through His blood (Luke 22:20). It would be a covenant of forgiveness for all those who would trust in Him. And it would involve a true change of heart, a transformation from the inside out.

● ● ●

Anytime God is involved in a covenant, here's what we can bank on: He will do *everything* He's promised, because He *always* keeps His word. We can trust Him. The biblical covenants show that even when we're faithless, God remains faithful. He cannot—and will not—deny himself (2 Timothy 2:13).

• • •

As you pray today, do so in the strength of this truth: the God you are talking to is a covenant-making, promise-keeping God.

ANGRY

Displeasure over things that are and shouldn't be,
or things that aren't and should be

Restore us to yourself, LORD, that we may return; renew our days as of old
unless you have utterly rejected us and are angry with us beyond measure.
(LAMENTATIONS 5:21–22)

Everywhere we look people are hot under the collar, smoldering, ready to blow.

We witness parking lot rage. Workplace rage. Restaurant rage. We've got travelers melting down on flights. Our social media feeds are filled with those who know how to USE THAT CAPS LOCK KEY TO SHOW THE WORLD HOW TICKED OFF THEY REALLY ARE!!!!

Regrettably, we sometimes see embarrassing anger in ourselves. In rush-hour traffic (there's an oxymoron for you!), we find ourselves creeping along at the pace of an elderly snail. A fellow commuter speeds up to *three* whole miles per hour and zooms in front of us, delaying us for at least five whole *seconds*. In a zeptosecond (google it), we go from 0 to 100 on the old fury scale.

What is up with all this rage? And what do we do with Bible passages that talk about God being angry with His people?

• • •

When the prophet Jeremiah watched Jerusalem fall to the invading Babylonians, he wept and attributed this judgment to God being angry over the sins of His people. Jeremiah is not the only biblical writer to say such a thing. References to God's displeasure fill the Bible, and multiple Hebrew words are used. The most common is *ap*, which is translated "angry," but literally could be translated "nostril" or "face" (and may refer to the way humans sometimes flare their nostrils or get flushed in the face when angry). *Qatsaph*, the word used in Lamentations 5:22, is even stronger, conveying the idea of intense fury or wrath.

• • •

Is anything more cringeworthy than seeing people lose it, go off on others, and then try to justify themselves? Claims of righteous anger are invariably light on the righteous and heavy on the anger—except when it comes to God. Here's why: God is infinite and unchanging, He never ceases to be loving or patient, gracious or compassionate—even when He is furious over something that threatens to sully His name, hurt His people, or hinder His work.

If you heard about a hospital administrator angrily firing a surgeon for knowingly using unsterile equipment, you'd cheer, not criticize. Likewise, when God deals forcefully with some human (mis)behavior, it's because a strong response is warranted.

• • •

Getting angry over things that are and shouldn't be, or things that are not and should be, isn't inherently sinful. We know this because both God the Father (Numbers 12:9) and Christ the Son (Mark 3:5) are described in the Bible as feeling angry. Such passages show us that it's actually possible to be angry without sinning (Ephesians 4:26) and challenge us to channel that anger in productive directions.

Tell God you want that kind of anger only—holy displeasure against unholy things.

45

GLORY

Weightiness, heaviness, or worthiness

Then the man brought me by way of the north gate to the front of the temple.
I looked and saw the glory of the LORD filling the temple of the LORD,
and I fell facedown. (EZEKIEL 44:4)

People speak of glorious dinners, vacations, and sunsets. They take selfies at the rim of the Grand Canyon, then post them on social media with the caption "Glorious!"

In the Bible, however, when people catch a glimpse of divine glory—or when it comes crashing down on their heads—they inevitably do what the prophet Ezekiel did in the verse cited above.

They fall on their faces.

● ● ●

The Hebrew word translated "glory" literally means "heavy" (as opposed to light and inconsequential).* No wonder when God shows up in dramatic ways, people find themselves prostrate and breathless. How could it be otherwise? God is the most substantive reality of all. His glory is weighty! Who can stand in the

---

*The Hebrew word translated "glory" is *kabod.*

presence of infinite brightness and brilliance, unbounded greatness and goodness?

We use terms like these: Grandeur. Magnificence. Majesty. Impressiveness. Worthiness. Splendor. Beauty. Perfection. All fine, respectable words, but none is up to the task of capturing the essence of the glory of God. No thesaurus—no warehouse full of thesauruses—can properly capture it.

So the Bible describes it—or tries to. It tells of God's glory being manifested to Israel as an overwhelming cloud, a breathtaking pillar of fire, divine pyrotechnics on the top of Mount Sinai. Isaiah wrote of how he collapsed under the awesome weight of God's glorious presence as the temple filled with smoke.

Here's a fun project. Read the story of God's people and count how many times you see the word *facedown*.

● ● ●

Glory is a major Bible theme. The word is found in its various forms roughly 375 times in the Old Testament, 25 times in Ezekiel alone. People of wealth or reputation are sometimes described by our culture as having a certain glory. But this is pitiful in the dazzling light of the One who made our world and sustains and permeates it (Psalm 19:1).

Why don't we see this divine glory more often? It could be that we're not paying attention. Maybe, like Moses in his encounter with God at Sinai's "burning bush," we need to keep our eyes peeled and be quicker to turn aside to investigate unusual happenings (Exodus 3:2–3). If his experience is any indicator, this much is true: a holy curiosity yields glorious results.

● ● ●

Since "the whole earth is full of his glory" (Isaiah 6:3), ask "the Lord of glory" (1 Corinthians 2:8) for eyes to see. And ponder this: if you're a child of God through faith in Christ, He, in all His glory and weightiness, lives *inside you*. How did Paul put it? "Christ in you, the hope of glory" (Colossians 1:27).

The staggering fact of God's glory is hard to fully grasp but at the very least it ought to prompt this question: "What business do I have living a light, inconsequential life?"

DREEAM

A set of images, thoughts, and/or feelings during sleep by
which God has, at times, communicated His will

In the first year of Belshazzar king of Babylon, Daniel had a dream,
and visions passed through his mind as he was lying in bed.
He wrote down the substance of his dream. (DANIEL 7:1)

Dr. Martin Luther King Jr. had a dream that shook a nation.
Fantine, the poor girl in the Broadway version of *Les
Misérables* sang about a dream so gut-wrenching it had audience
members reaching for their antidepressants.

Meanwhile, your dreams—they're just *weird*. Last night you
were running down Main Street in your birthday suit being
chased by a giant waffle. Thank God you woke up right as you got
to that cliff overlooking an ocean of maple syrup.

Dreams are as old as the human race, which may be why, in the
great story of God, they're so prominent. Dreams were one of the
"various ways" (Hebrews 1:1) that God sometimes spoke to people, revealing His will or what He was planning to do (Genesis
20:3–6; 28:12; 31:24; 37:5–10; 1 Kings 3:5; Matthew 1:20; 2:12,
19–22). God routinely communicated to His prophets through
dreams (Numbers 12:4–6) and visions. In addition, God gave
others—Joseph and Daniel, for example—the ability to make
sense of puzzling, highly symbolic dreams.

• • •

The Hebrew verb meaning "to dream" sometimes has the meaning "to being strong or healthy."* Scholars aren't sure why, or what to make of this connection.

Here's what we do know: In the Bible dreams are often mentioned in connection with visions (Job 7:14; Daniel 1:17; Joel 2:28; Zechariah 10:2). Probably the word *visions* is meant to distinguish separate vivid scenes within a longer dream.

• • •

Our normal, regular dreams (for example, those that have us running from giant waffles) are simply the function of our brains doing what our brains were designed to do. Neuroscientists tell us that dreaming is how we subconsciously try to process life events and our emotional responses to them. At the very least, dreams show the marvelous complexity of human nature. Physiologically and emotionally speaking, we are indeed "fearfully and wonderfully made" (Psalm 139:14).

Divine dreams (those given by God in order to reveal His plan) show the Creator's gracious desire to communicate with His creatures. His heart is to draw people to himself.

• • •

Does God *still* speak to people through dreams? Consider the growing number of credible reports from those in non-Christian cultures claiming they've seen and heard Jesus in their dreams, saying things like, "I am the way, the truth, and the life."

Without question dreams are mysterious, sometimes weird (giant waffles, anyone?), and open to wildly divergent interpretations. But when a dream features Jesus, living Word of God, saying things that align with—and are found in—the written Word

---

Chalam is the Hebrew word for *dream*.

of God in order to call people to himself, that's a dream that ought to shake—and wake—us up.

CHANGED

To be turned upside down

How can I give you up, Ephraim? How can I hand you over, Israel? . . .
My heart is changed within me; all my compassion is aroused.
(HOSEA 11:8)

Lots of people—far too many, in fact—think of God as stony and unfeeling, His personality somewhere between *Star Trek*'s Mr. Spock and one of those expressionless guards in front of Buckingham Palace.

Those people are in for a rude, theological awakening when they get to the Old Testament book of Hosea.

Hosea, if you've forgotten, was the Jewish prophet told by God to do the unthinkable: "Go, marry a promiscuous woman and have children with her" (Hosea 1:2). The reason for this outrageous command? To hold up a mirror to the nation of Israel. To give God's chosen people a scandalous picture of their own spiritual unfaithfulness.

Hosea, God love him, swallowed hard and said, "Okay."

It was a stunning directive to be sure, but there's an even bigger shock. Read the whole story and note what it reveals about the Lord. This isn't God, the passionless lawgiver. This is God, the shattered spouse. In Hosea, God is hurt and heartbroken. He feels angry and betrayed—just as every victim of adultery does.

Ready to give His people their walking papers one moment, lamenting His inability to let them go the next, He finally cries, "My heart is *changed* within me" (11:8).

• • •

The Hebrew verb describing God's heart here as "changed" is elsewhere rendered "torn" (NLT), "turned" (KJV), or "turned over" (NASB). It is translated "recoils" in the ESV.

This colorful word is *haphak*, and it is used in its various forms more than a hundred times in the Old Testament. It's used to describe a feeling of weakness (Psalm 32:4) or being overwhelmed (Job 30:15). It describes a town being overthrown (Genesis 19:21) or destroyed (Lamentations 4:6), a loaf of bread tumbling down a hill (Judges 7:13), a hair turning white (Leviticus 13:3), a heart that's flipped upside down (Lamentations 1:20).

• • •

In a few places, the Bible *seems* to suggest that God changes His mind (in addition to this verse in Hosea, see Genesis 6:6 and Exodus 32:14). Other passages insist that He does not because He is unchanging (Numbers 23:19; Malachi 3:6; James 1:17).

The idea in Hosea isn't to portray God as wishy-washy or vacillating. It's to demonstrate that He's personal. He has feelings. What's more, He's relational—wholly committed to those He loves. Therefore, when God's covenant people chase after other lovers, they're not just breaking some arbitrary law; they're breaking His heart.

• • •

Two questions to ponder: (1) How does it alter your view of God to see Him as the book of Hosea describes Him? (2) In what ways, if any, is reading the story of Hosea like looking in the mirror for you?

DAY

The temporal canvas on which God and humanity
paint the Great Story of the world

The sun will be turned to darkness and the moon to blood before the
coming of the great and dreadful day of the LORD. (JOEL 2:31)

Pulitzer Prize-winning author Annie Dillard once observed,
"How we spend our days is, of course, how we spend our lives."

Maybe this oft-forgotten truth explains why the Bible has so
much to say about days.

"In the beginning" God created days (Genesis 1). He made
six days per week for working and being productive, and one
more—known as the Sabbath—for resting and being reflective.
Across the Hebrew calendar, God sprinkled other "holy" days
during which his people were to engage in special feasts and
remembrances.

When you think about it, the Bible is essentially a record
of real events—both miraculous and mundane—that took place
on actual days . . . days just like today.

• • •

The Hebrew word for "day" is *yom*. (Perhaps you've heard references to Yom Kippur, which means "Day of Atonement"—the

holiest day on the Jewish calendar.) *Yom* is found more than two thousand times in the Old Testament and refers to a unit of time—usually to an actual, 24-hour solar day—but sometimes to an unspecified length of time (Genesis 2:4; Ephesians 6:13; Hebrews 3:8).

In the writings of the prophets, we see multiple references to "the day of the LORD" (Isaiah 13:6; Ezekiel 30:3; Joel 2:11; Amos 5:18; Zephaniah 1:14), clearly a future day of calamity and divine judgment. The message of both the Old Testament prophets and the New Testament apostles is essentially, "Live today with that future day in mind."

His talk of a dreadful day aside, Joel also spoke of a coming day of restoration for the people of God (Joel 3:18).

• • •

King David pointed out that God ordains for each of us a specific number of days of life—no more and no less (Psalm 139:16). Probably in light of this truth—that is, how fleeting life is—Moses made this request of God: "Teach us to number our days, that we may gain a heart of wisdom" (Psalm 90:12).

Have you ever done that—numbered your days? Currently the average life expectancy for Americans is just under seventy-nine years. That means—if you're average—all your good, bad, and ho-hum days together, all those birthdays and school days, workdays and holidays, sick days and vacation days will tally about 28,750.

That sounds like a lot until we remember that time flies and the days tend to run together.

• • •

Each morning we have a choice:

We can spend our precious hours till bedtime just trying to "get through the day." We can focus unhealthily on days gone by or fret unhelpfully over days to come (that God, in fact, hasn't even promised to give us).

Or we can see the new day for what it is: a precious gift made and ordained by God and unique in the history of the world. We can rejoice and be glad in it (Psalm 118:24). And we can attempt great things with and for God.

When we think about our days in that light, it's not a hard choice.

HEAR

To pay attention with a view toward
doing what is required

Hear this word, Israel, this lament I take up concerning you.

(Amos 5:1)

Why are most of us so bad at listening? Can we blame our smartphones, or do we chalk up our distraction to the fact that this supremely important skill isn't taught in our schools? Maybe it's because we have so few role models? Or it's that we live in a hyperactive age that champions multitasking as a way of staying ahead of the proverbial train?

We're becoming competent at so many things. Listening is not, for most people, one of those things. This is especially sad when we consider how many problems, national and personal, are caused by a simple failure to really hear (and heed) what others are saying.

• • •

Would it shock you to discover that the Bible makes a big fuss over our need to perk up and pay careful attention? Especially our need to hear and obey God?

The Hebrew verb translated "hear" is *shama*, and we find it more than 1,100 times in the Old Testament! *Shama* refers to a kind of hearing that transcends physiology. In fact, it's *after* the sound vibrations of someone's voice move through our ossicles (the tiny bones in the middle ear) to our cochlea (located in the inner ear), where they are converted into nerve signals and sent to our brain for interpretation, that biblical hearing begins.

Shama means to hear with intention, interest, and a will to obey. It means, in our vernacular, to "get the message" and adjust one's life accordingly.

● ● ●

It's one thing to absorb a bunch of religious facts in a Sunday school or catechism class. But nodding at, discussing, memorizing, and even parroting spiritual truths is not the same as *hearing* them. Hearing—in the biblical sense—implies doing. It's synonymous with obedience. This is why we read verses like this: "Hear, Israel, *and be careful to obey* so that it may go well with you . . ." (Deuteronomy 6:3 Emphasis added)

● ● ●

In the Gospels, Jesus often concludes a time of teaching with the curious invitation, "If anyone has ears to hear, let them hear" (Mark 4:23). What an odd expression! "Ears to hear"? What else are ears for? This is the master teacher's way of saying that *knowing what to do* and *doing what we know* are two entirely different things.

Practice being a better listener today. When you're with others, put your smartphone in your pocket. Make eye contact. Block out other distractions. Don't just nod mindlessly. Focus on what's being said—not just the words but the heart behind them.

Do this with people—and *especially* with God. Hear God's voice with a heart that says, "I will do whatever you say."

PRIDE

Elevating one's self in order to look down on others

The pride of your heart has deceived you, you who live in the clefts of
the rocks and make your home on the heights, you who say to yourself,
"Who can bring me down to the ground?" (OBADIAH 1:3)

In the biggest game of the year, the cocky team with the smug
coach and the trash-talking quarterback gets drubbed. Millions of sports fans take immense pleasure in their humiliation.

In a televised town hall meeting, a pompous, condescending
politician is taken down a few pegs by an unassuming factory
worker. The audience cheers wildly.

Clearly, if there's one thing people can't stand, it's someone
who's arrogant.

And, in the epic story of life, God despises pride even more
than we do.

• • •

There are multiple Hebrew words that get translated "pride" in the
Old Testament. The most common one comes from a root word
that means "to rise up."* The connotation is almost always negative (see Proverbs 16:18), picturing someone who is trying to

---

*The most common Hebrew word for *pride* is *gaown*.

ascend or climb over others, a person seeking to exalt him or her-
self. Another Hebrew word means "height." Another, used in Job
41:34, may convey the idea of "strutting about." Yet another refers
to "arrogance" or "exaggerated self-importance" (Proverbs 11:2)
that results in a contemptuous, disdainful attitude toward others.*

It's from these sorts of words and their "lofty" meanings that
we derive all those colorful phrases we use to describe proud people: "high and mighty," "stuck up," "highfalutin," "looking down
his nose," "uppity," "on her high horse."

Do you see? Pride is all about elevating oneself.

• • •

So why did God tell Obadiah to prophesy against Edom?
Here's a quick Old Testament history review: The Edomites
were descendants of Esau. The Israelites were descendants of
Esau's twin brother, Jacob. The two nations were related—from
the same family tree. They should have been allies.

Far from it. When the Israelites were wandering in the wilderness, Edom angrily refused to show any sort of hospitality
(Numbers 20:14–21). Later, when Israel was being attacked by
unspecified neighbors, Edom joined in the assault! According
to the book of Obadiah, the Edomites gloated over Israel's mis-
fortune (vv. 10–14). Not only that, but they enjoyed looking
down from Petra, their capital city situated in the mountains of
modern-day Jordan, and thinking, *No one can touch us* (see Jeremiah 48:29).

God's response was along the lines of "Oh, really? Watch
this."

• • •

---

* *Gobah* means "height." *Shachats* is the word in Job 41:34 that may suggest the idea of strutting
about. *Zadown* is arrogance or exaggerated self-importance in Proverbs 11:2.

All the way through the Bible it's clear that God hates pride (Proverbs 8:13; 16:5; 2 Timothy 3:2). When it rears its head, He opposes it fiercely (Proverbs 15:25; Ezekiel 28:17; Romans 12:16). On the other hand, those who are humble—who lower themselves rather than vaunt themselves—always find grace (James 4:6; 1 Peter 5:5).

C. S. Lewis warned that as long as we're looking down on others, we can't see the One who's high above us. Look up in humility. Ask the Lord to show you where you need to come back down to earth.

APPOINTED

Assigned, provided, or ordained

And the LORD appointed a great fish to swallow Jonah,
and Jonah was in the stomach of the fish three days and three nights.
(JONAH 1:17 NASB)

Deism is the belief system—wildly popular in the seventeenth and eighteenth centuries—that says God made the world and promptly disappeared. Is this because the Almighty is shy? Impersonal? Off creating other galaxies? Deists don't focus much on the why, only the what: "God is *not* involved in human affairs," they insist. "You want miracles? Answered prayers? Don't hold your breath," a deist would tell you.

Maybe if the prophet Jonah could talk to a deist, he'd smile and reply, " 'Don't hold your breath'—good one! That's *exactly* what I ended up doing in the depths of the Mediterranean, after God got extremely involved in my life."

• • •

The Jewish prophet Jonah was told by the very non-deistic God of the Bible to go to Nineveh and tell the Assyrians to repent.

Only one problem: Assyria was a godless empire determined to destroy Israel! Not wanting to see his enemies experience God's mercy, Jonah promptly boarded a boat going the opposite direction.

This is when God began appointing various things. The Hebrew word for "appoint" sometimes refers to numbering or counting something (2 Kings 12:11). But it can also mean to determine or destine something (see Isaiah 65:12), to assign, provide, or ordain a thing.*

The book of Jonah says that after God sent a storm (1:4) to get the attention of Jonah—and after the prophet convinced his fellow travelers to toss him in the sea—God appointed a fish to swallow him (1:17). Three days later, when Jonah decided he might be better off obeying after all, the Lord commanded the fish to vomit Jonah onto dry land (2:10).

The waterlogged prophet reluctantly carried out his mission, and—just as he feared—the Ninevites repented. When Jonah began sulking, God meddled even more in His servant's life. He appointed a plant to grow and give Jonah temporary shade (4:6), appointed a worm to come eat the plant (4:7), then appointed a scorching east wind to make Jonah faint (4:8).

Does all that sound like deism to you?

● ● ●

God is the opposite of disinterested and distracted! The picture painted in Jonah (and throughout the Bible) is of a God who's highly engaged.

We often speak of coincidence and happenstance. We need to talk more about providence. God is the great orchestrator of life, the ingenious director of the human drama in which we are all players. The biblical testimony is that God is intricately involved in the affairs of humanity, coordinating all things to bring about His good purposes (Psalms 115:3; 135:6; Proverbs 16:9; Isaiah 14:24–27; Ephesians 1:11–12).

---

* *Appoint* is *manah* in Hebrew.

• • •

Even if you're not technically a deist, are you living like one? Are you looking for God? Expecting Him to show up in your life?

If not, why not?

JUSTICE

The standard by which rewards and punishments
are rightly administered

But as for me, I am filled with power, with the Spirit of the LORD, and with
justice and might, to declare to Jacob his transgression, to Israel his sin.

(MICAH 3:8)

Elected officials exempt themselves from a new law that will
adversely affect most voters. A corrupt CEO is fired for being
a total creep at best, a criminal at worst. On his way out the door,
he gets a multimillion-dollar severance package. A homeless vet-
eran is brutally beaten by a group of youths while some of their
peers laugh, cheer, and record video.

I bet almost daily you find yourself muttering, "That's *so* wrong!
Where's the justice?"

If so, you know a bit of how the ancient Jewish prophets felt.

• • •

Justice is a major theme in God's story because injustice is ram-
pant in our sin-plagued, broken world. People embrace ideas like
"Might makes right" and "If I *can* do it, I *will* do it" (never mind
if an action is right or hurtful to others). Such people end up taking
care of their own—and taking advantage of all the rest.

The Hebrew word for "justice" is a broad term with wide application.[*] Since it involves exercising a kind of holy discernment—distinguishing between right and wrong—it first requires a divine compass where God's law is true north. Using this compass, rendering fair and impartial verdicts (Deuteronomy 25:1) becomes possible.

Biblical justice demands the punishment and the righting of every wrong. It champions the rights of victims: "The LORD works righteousness and justice for all the oppressed" (Psalm 103:6). It rebukes wrongdoers—especially those in power, as Micah and the other prophets did—and it exonerates the innocent. It denounces and seeks to dismantle unfair systems that give preference only to an elite few (Genesis 18:25). It doesn't just stop discrimination (Leviticus 19:15); it also attempts to show great kindness and compassion to those who have been mistreated or forgotten (Zechariah 7:9).

● ● ●

Do we really need to explain why justice is important? If you've ever been on the receiving end of injustice, you know how crucial justice is.

Golden Rule, anyone?

● ● ●

Maybe in reading the Bible, you've never noticed how prominent the idea of justice is. This could be due to the fact that you've not spent much time in the prophets (they harp on the idea even more than the other books). Or, it could be because related words to this idea of justice are sometimes translated as "judgment" or "righteousness."

---

[*]The Hebrew word for *justice* is *mishpat.*

Know this: God demands justice on the part of His human creatures because He himself is just (Deuteronomy 32:4). He *loves* justice (Psalm 11:7; Isaiah 61:8).

Ask Him to work in your heart in such a way that, more and more, you see people and situations as He does. And that you act as He would act, if He were in your shoes.

JEALOUS

A passionate desire for exclusivity within
a committed relationship

The LORD is a jealous and avenging God; the LORD takes vengeance and
is filled with wrath. The LORD takes vengeance on his foes and vents his
wrath against his enemies. (NAHUM 1:2)

Agrowing number of people in contemporary culture practice "open relationships" and even "open marriages." This is
where a couple enters into a relationship but then grants each
other permission to be intimate with anyone else they happen to
meet and like. One-night stands? Sleeping with coworkers? No
problem, because open relationships are rooted in consensual
non-monogamy. The old marital vow about "forsaking all others"? Forget it. In an open relationship no such expectations exist
because no such restrictions exist.

This odd phenomenon raises multiple questions, but the most
obvious one is, don't people in such relationships get jealous,
at least sometimes?

You bet they do.

• • •

In the Old Testament, God is described several times as being
jealous (Exodus 20:5; Deuteronomy 32:21; Ezekiel 16:42). The

Hebrew word suggests zeal mixed with passion. Jealousy therefore is a consuming desire for exclusivity in a relationship and a fierce commitment to protect what is one's own.[*]

We nod when the Bible says that God is "holy" and "loving." The adjective "jealous," however, makes us wince. It shouldn't. From the beginning, the people of God willingly committed to enter into an exclusive relationship with the Almighty. They agreed to His up-front terms of "no other gods" (Exodus 20:3; 24:3). They later promised to love the Lord with *all* their hearts and souls—not just part of their hearts, and not just on days they weren't flirting with some other deity (Deuteronomy 6:5).

• • •

A careful reading of Scripture shows that God isn't jealous like some unhinged stalker on social media. He doesn't force anyone to be in a relationship with Him. However, those who say by faith they want to be His people can't also have other loves and engage in flings whenever the whim strikes.

In a sense, *this* was the reason God sent the prophets—and it was their primary message: God never has, and never will, settle for an open relationship with His people.

• • •

Desiring things that don't belong to you—another's wealth or looks, let's say—that's sinful jealousy. That's being jealous *of* someone (Genesis 30:1; 37:11). Wanting good things—the exclusive love of a spouse, for example—that's a pure jealousy. That's being jealous *for* someone or something.

When you think about it, God *has* to be jealous for His people. Imagine if He were to say, "Go ahead. Give yourself to other loves.

---

[*] *Jealous* is *qana* in Hebrew.

I don't care." In that case God would essentially be saying, "Other things are just as deserving of your attention and affection as I am." That idea, of course, is a lie, and God cannot lie. His holy nature means He could never suggest or sanction an evil thing.

Enough pondering. Let's make this personal. God is jealous *for you*. He wants your whole heart.

Does He have it?

WOE

An expression of grief or displeasure

Woe to him who says to wood, "Come to life!" Or to lifeless stone, "Wake up!" Can it give guidance? It is covered with gold and silver; there is no breath in it. (HABAKKUK 2:19)

Y̶ou have to hand it to those Old Testaments prophets. Talk about ice water in the old veins. They were fearless: staring down kings, religious leaders, and neighbors, then delivering God's hard, uncomfortable truth.

Wait. On second thought, is that even true? Fearless? Surely the prophets had at least a few unnerving moments when it dawned on them, *If I say everything that God has told me to say here, things will* not *go well for me.*

Well, if they felt such fear, it didn't stop them from doing their jobs (Jonah notwithstanding). After a few deep breaths, they opened their mouths wide and spoke the unpopular messages they'd been given to speak.

And you could always tell when a message was especially bleak—the prophet would pepper it with the word *woe.*

• • •

Woe is a cry of mourning, displeasure, or disgust. It's *hoy* in Hebrew. (You've probably heard a Jewish person exclaim, "Oy!"

or "Oy vey!") It conveys the idea of "Alas!" or "Ah!" or "Oh!" It's typically delivered with great passion, a pained, almost haunted expression, a shake of the head.

We find the word *woe* a handful of times in the historical and poetic books of the Old Testament—it's common in passages where people are grieving a death (1 Kings 13:30). Mostly the word is found in the prophetic books—where God's spokespeople are warning of imminent judgment. *Woe* was one of Jesus's go-to words when speaking to Israel's religious leaders (see Matthew 23).

• • •

Some people feel woe over social media and the unknown ways it's affecting our souls—and the soul of a culture. We won't likely know the full truth for some years, but one of the things it's obviously doing is conditioning people to post only content that will generate lots of "likes" and "shares."

And the people who dare to share uncomfortable or unpopular truths—the people who cry "woe!" about wrong things in our culture? They get "unfollowed," "blocked," or "unfriended." (Of course, this also happens to people who are simply rude or obnoxious.)

• • •

Here's a good exercise. Look up the hundred or so verses in the Bible that use this word, and make a list of the things that elicit God's displeasure. Then ask yourself, *Am I guilty of doing these things?*

Somebody once said, "When you realize you're on a path to woe, it's time to say, 'Whoa!'" Sure, it's a corny little quip, but it's true—and maybe something we can remember.

GATHER

To collect things or assemble people
for a specific reason

"At that time I will gather you; at that time I will bring you home. I will give you honor and praise among all the peoples of the earth when I restore your fortunes before your very eyes," says the LORD. (ZEPHANIAH 3:20)

Even if we moderns aren't true hunter-gatherers, we're at least gatherers. We gather for meetings on workdays, gather with loved ones on holidays, gather up all the dirty clothes on laundry day. When bad days come, we gather up our courage—or start gathering excuses.

Guess what? There's a lot of gathering in the story of God too. Among other things, Bible people gathered stones (Genesis 31:46), money (Genesis 47:14), straw (Exodus 5:7), the harvest they planted (Leviticus 23:22), the heavenly bread given them by God (Exodus 16:4). They gathered to fight (Joshua 9:2; Judges 11:20) and to participate in religious ceremonies (1 Samuel 7:5). When a man died in the Bible, he was described as having been "gathered to his people" (Genesis 25:17).

In the New Testament, after one of His miraculous feedings, Jesus instructed His disciples to gather the leftover pieces (John 6:12). Imagine that—leftovers are biblical!

• • •

Several Hebrew words can be (and are) translated "gather" in the Old Testament. The one used by Zephaniah in the verse above is *qabas* and has the idea of assembling. It's related to *qibbus*, from which we derive the word *kibbutz*. (A kibbutz is an Israeli communal settlement, a gathering of people who live and work together.)

In the New Testament, the primary Greek verb translated "gather" is *synago*, from which we get the word *synagogue*, a Jewish assembly or congregation.

• • •

Again and again, the Bible shows God to be the ultimate Gatherer. Like Zephaniah, Jeremiah reveals the Lord's gracious plans for His rebellious people: " 'I will gather you from all the nations and places where I have banished you,' declares the LORD, 'and will bring you back to the place from which I carried you into exile' " (Jeremiah 29:14). This regathering is repeatedly described in Scripture as a prelude to unimaginable blessing (Micah 4:6; Zephaniah 3:19–20).

Isaiah spoke of a coming Servant (see chapter 42) of God who would gather the lambs of His flock and gently lead them (Isaiah 40:11). Jesus, the man identified by the gospel writers as that prophesied Servant, spoke mournfully of His desire to gather the people of Jerusalem, "just as a hen gathers her brood under her wings" (Luke 13:34 NASB).

Other passages show God gathering the wicked for a wholly different reason: judgment (Joel 3:2; Zephaniah 2:1; 3:8; Revelation 20:8).

• • •

If your life feels like a scattered mess today, take comfort in the truth that God is a Gatherer. He specializes in finding all the broken pieces and bringing them together into a beautiful whole.

He will do that for you if you ask Him.

STIR UP

To incite to action

So the LORD stirred up the spirit of Zerubbabel son of Shealtiel, governor of Judah, and the spirit of Joshua son of Jozadak, the high priest, and the spirit of the whole remnant of the people. They came and began to work on the house of the LORD Almighty, their God. (HAGGAI 1:14)

Even a first grader knows that life can be a beatdown. And when hope slips away, discouragement knows how to find its way in through the cracks. In such times, our tendency is to pull back and start going through the motions. Before we know it, we're on autopilot. Soon we've got a bad case of spiritual narcolepsy. We're sleepwalking our lives away!

This was the experience of the group of Jews who had returned eagerly to Jerusalem following the Babylonian exile. On the front end, talk of "being back home" and "rebuilding the temple" sparked big grins, enthusiastic whoops, and high fives all around. Sixteen years later, such phrases resulted in eye rolls and yawns.

Around 520 BC, God responded. He gave His prophet Haggai a short but blunt message intended to stir up the demoralized populace.

• • •

Okay, okay, *stir up* is two words in English. True. In Hebrew, however, it's only one—the verb *ya'ar*. *Ya'ar* means "to alert or rouse or awaken." In Haggai's case this wake-up call involved a curious cocktail of divine words: a pointed question, a sobering challenge—repeated twice!—to "give careful thought to your ways" (vv. 5, 7), and the comforting reassurance, "'I am with you,' declares the LORD" (v. 13).

The result? Wide eyes. Trembling hands. Racing hearts. The Lord stirred up everyone who heard Haggai's holy message—Zerubbabel the governor, Joshua the high priest, and "the whole remnant of the people" (v. 14).

• • •

Being stirred up is more than getting goose bumps—it's being jolted back to reality *and* spurred to action. Notice that, as a result of Haggai speaking the very words of God, both leaders and regular folks "came and began to work on the house of the LORD Almighty, their God" (v. 14).

This phenomenon—which happens repeatedly throughout the Bible—reminds us that God shakes slumbering hearts awake. He uses His Word and His people to jar sluggish souls.

• • •

In his books and sermons, the eighteenth-century preacher and author George MacDonald often discussed this idea of needing to be roused or awakened from spiritual drowsiness. One of the old soul's prayers was "Lord, wake me oftener, lest I sin."[*] In another place he spoke of the need to wake our souls "unnumbered times a day."[†] Translation: we need to be stirred up!

If *ya'ar* battling lethargy of the soul (a little Hebrew pun there, just to make sure you're tracking), ask God to send a Haggai into your life. Sometimes all we need is someone who will, without apology, declare the truth of God to our slumbering hearts.

[*] George MacDonald, *Diary of an Old Soul* (Minneapolis: Augsburg Publishing House, 1994), 24.
[†] MacDonald, *Diary*, 55.

ANGEL

A supernatural messenger-servant of God

While the angel who was speaking to me was leaving,
another angel came to meet him. (ZECHARIAH 2:3)

A tour through the Bible that didn't include a brief look at angels would be like a tour of J. R. R. Tolkien's Middle-earth that failed to mention hobbits, elves, or dwarves.

Angels play a major role in the great story of God. Consequently, they pop up everywhere in Scripture—like the time an angel brought the prophet Zechariah an urgent message from God. The gist? The people of Jerusalem needed to get busy and finish rebuilding the temple! Why? Because one day Messiah's glory would fill it!

• • •

The Hebrew word for "angel" is *malak*, which means "messenger." (It's *angelos* in New Testament Greek.) An angel, then, is a heavenly courier, a servant of God who brings communiqués from God. That's not what all angels do, but that's the primary meaning of the word.

Occasionally in the Old Testament, human messengers (1 Samuel 6:21) or prophets (2 Chronicles 36:15–16) are called by this word. Our focus here, however, is on the heavenly messengers that appear throughout Scripture—the supernatural beings that do God's bidding.

Angels offer praise to God (Isaiah 6:3). They are said to protect and guide God's people (Genesis 19:12–17; Exodus 23:20).
They are shown ministering to God's servants (1 Kings 19; Matthew 4:11). They are described as executing God's judgment
(Psalm 78:49). It's worth noting that typically in Scripture, when
angels show up, onlookers very nearly need CPR. (In other words,
when Raphael painted all his cute, chubby, childlike cherubs, he
was taking major artistic license!)

We see angels in Jacob's dream of the staircase that ascended
into heaven (Genesis 28:12). They are active leading up to the
birth of Christ (Luke 1–2) and on hand to interpret the empty
tomb to Jesus's confused followers.

• • •

The presence of angels in the story of God reveals so much: that
there's more to this life than what we can usually see, that heaven
and earth *do* commingle—that God is serious about getting important messages to His creatures.

Jesus once made a comment about children having angels
in heaven (Matthew 18:10). Whatever you believe about "guardian angels," the Bible does say cryptically, "Do not forget to show
hospitality to strangers, for by so doing some people have shown
hospitality to angels without knowing it" (Hebrews 13:2).

• • •

If you've been hoping to become an angel when you die and trying
hard to "earn your wings" . . . hate to break it to you, but that's an idea
from the movies, not from the Bible.

However, there is this: when we deliver messages from God,
we are, in a literal sense, being angelic.

Maybe we could devote ourselves to that.

HOW?

A word used by questioners, either to gain
understanding or to argue

"I have loved you," says the LORD. "But you ask,
'How have you loved us?'" (MALACHI 1:2)

People who have spent big chunks of their lives trying to understand what it means to walk (see chapter 23) with God know all about the dark side of faith. They've experienced moments—maybe even whole seasons—of doubt. Most have had bouts of spiritual apathy.

When we find ourselves in such places, when we're yawning in the face of great spiritual truths, or when we find our hearts growing cold, or when it's clear we'd rather argue with God than obey Him, how should we respond?

We should look at Malachi, that's how.

• • •

Malachi's prophecy is the final book of the Old Testament. Six different times in its three short chapters, the jaded Israelites respond to God's announcements by asking "How?" "*How* have you loved us?" (1:2). "*How* have we shown contempt for your name?" (1:6). "*How* have we defiled you?" (1:7). "*How* have we wearied [you]?" (2:17). "*How* are we to return?" (3:7). "*How* are we robbing you?" (3:8).

"How" is the translation of the interrogative Hebrew pronoun *ma*. Depending on the context, it can also be translated "what" or "why."

This particle is worth pondering, not because its etymology is amazing, but because of what it reveals about the ones using it and, more importantly, about the One to whom it is continually addressed.

• • •

When we catch ourselves bombarding heaven with questions that begin with the word *how*, we are wise to take a closer look at our hearts.

Sometimes our *how* questions are innocent and prompted by a sense of wonder (Luke 1:34) or confusion (John 1:48; 3:9). On other occasions we may be weary of suffering, and like the suffering psalmist, simply asking, "How long, LORD, how long?" (Psalm 6:3; see also 13:1–2; 35:17; 79:5; 80:4; 89:46; Habakkuk 1:2).

But oftentimes our *how* questions come from hearts that are skeptical (John 7:41; 9:16; 10:24). In such times, we want to argue more than understand. We're being ornery, not open, hard-hearted, not humble. Think of a defiant, mouthy teenager who won't listen and just wants to lash out.

• • •

When you find yourself asking God the kind of *how* questions that are rooted more in a frustrated desire to push Him away than a desperate attempt to understand, how should you respond? Here's how: Make the painfully honest prayer of Teresa of Avila your own: "Oh God, I don't love you. I don't even want to love you. But I want to want to love you."

59

JESUS

A proper name that means
"Jehovah is salvation" or "the LORD saves"

She will give birth to a son, and you are to give him the name Jesus,
because he will save his people from their sins. (MATTHEW 1:21)

Unless you're an angel (highly doubtful) or somehow reading this book from heaven (even more doubtful), you need rescue *right now* from at least one of the following:

Apathy
Lust
Depression
Guilt
Regret
Impure motives
Fear of ___
Anger
A wrong belief
An addictive habit
Envy
Shame
A powerful temptation
An unwise plan
Self-pity

Pride
Unemployment
A sticky situation
Debt
Greed
Worry
Purposelessness
Impatience
A parenting dilemma
A soul-killing job
Discouragement
People-pleasing
Gluttony
A toxic relationship
A critical spirit
Selfishness
Doubt
Hypocrisy
Bitterness
Exhaustion
A broken heart
Loneliness
Graceless religion
Materialism
Hopelessness

The fact is, there's not a day that goes by that we don't need some kind of saving.

Enter *Jesus*.

• • •

The angel Gabriel sat Joseph down. After explaining that the baby boy growing in Mary's womb had been conceived by the Holy Spirit, he issued the divine command, "Give him the name Jesus."

Jesus means "the Lord saves." It was a common name in ancient Palestine, the Greek equivalent of the Hebrew name Joshua. (And, in fact, the King James Bible, in discussing the Old Testament character Joshua in Acts 7:45 and Hebrews 4:8, refers to Him as "Jesus.")

Such genius! Every time the name Jesus is spoken—whether yelled when people are angry or called when folks are in agony—it's a reminder that the world needs—that *we* need—rescue from sin and all its terrible consequences.

● ● ●

The Bible's claim that there's power in the name of Jesus (Luke 10:17; John 14:13; Acts 4:12, 30; Romans 10:13) doesn't mean we turn His name into an incantation, like a Vegas performer exclaiming, "Abracadabra!" Jesus's power is experienced by people who call on Him and trust Him from their hearts—not by those who mindlessly say His name with their mouths (Acts 19:13–17).

Jesus is "the name that is above every name." One day people will finally stop using His name as an expletive. Every mouth will acknowledge that He is Savior, Messiah, and Lord "to the glory of God the Father" (Philippians 2:9–11).

● ● ●

The Gospels show Jesus saving all kinds of people from all sorts of things. Meaning, no matter where you saw yourself in that list above, Jesus is well able to deliver *you*.

Here's a recommendation: memorize Peter's urgent cry—"Lord, save me!" (Matthew 14:30)—and take it with you everywhere.

You'll need it for sure.

60

KINGDOM

The territory or realm over which a king has authority

Repent, for the kingdom of heaven has come near.

(MATTHEW 3:2)

We use the suffix *-dom* to describe various situations. *Boredom*, for example, is what we label those times we feel disinterested and blah. *Freedom* denotes a state of liberty (like when school lets out for the summer). *Stardom* means a person has attained fame or celebrity status. Your neighbor who just adopted another rescue pup—that makes nine—lives in *dogdom*. You get the idea.

Which brings us to *kingdom*.

• • •

Hebrew and Greek words translated "kingdom" are found some 375 times in the Bible! It's no small topic. The first time we hear the word in the New Testament, it is on the lips of John the Baptist, the forerunner (or advance man) of Jesus.

When John, with his locust breath and camel-hair outfit, intensely shouted to the gawking crowds, "The *kingdom* of heaven has come near!" the implications should have been obvious. He was saying, in so many words, "People, listen up! God's heavenly rule has come to earth! The *kingdom* of heaven is near because the *king* of heaven is near!"

• • •

Since there are only a couple dozen monarchies left in the world—and most of those royals are mere figureheads with very little real power—it's hard for us to grasp the idea of a sovereign ruler who has real authority over every aspect of life. (Most of us can't even retain control over the TV remote for an entire evening!)

Yet the New Testament repeatedly whispers that Jesus is a king (Matthew 2:2; John 1:49; 12:13; 19:14). And not simply *a* king, but *the* King of kings (Revelation 19:16). When asked point blank if such talk was true, Jesus didn't bat an eye. He nodded His royal head (Matthew 27:11; John 18:37), accepted a crown (of thorns), and paid a king's ransom—His own life—for His subjects.

• • •

In teaching His followers how to pray, the unassuming King Jesus told them to say, "your kingdom come" (Matthew 6:10). This is a humble request for the righteous rule of God to fill the earth. It's a plea that people everywhere might gladly bow to the authority of the only King who is forever wise, eternally powerful, and infinitely good.

One day, every person *will* recognize Christ's right to rule. Every knee on earth *will* bow before Him (Philippians 2:10). Until that day, we can do four things: (1) rejoice with the psalmist that "the LORD Most High is awesome, the great King over all the earth" (Psalm 47:2); (2) bow to Christ's authority in our own lives; (3) work with Him to make our hearts fit for a king; and (4) introduce others to the good King with the common touch.

HELL

The final destiny of those who want nothing to do with God

And if your eye causes you to stumble, gouge it out and throw it away.
It is better for you to enter life with one eye than to have two eyes and be
thrown into the fire of hell. (MATTHEW 18:9)

If you asked people to make a list of bad words, many would cite infamous curse words. Others would mention distasteful words like *phlegm, vomit, ooze, pus, scab, mucus,* and *putrid*. (Are you wincing yet? Because that's a scowl-inducing list, for sure.)

Few would mention the four-letter word *hell*.

Despite its frequent use, the word *hell* is infrequently pondered. In July, a neighbor says it's "hot as hell." Come January, the same person remarks that it's "cold as hell." (Go figure.) A co-worker announces he's tired of the boss "making my life a living hell." Consequently, he is "mad as hell" and not going to take it anymore. In fact, he says, he's going to "raise hell" with upper management and keep at it even if there's not a "snowball's chance in hell" of success. And anyone who doesn't like it can "go to hell."

When it comes to ugly phrases, surely *that one* is the ugliest.

• • •

The primary Greek word translated "hell" in the New Testament is *gehenna*. It's derived from the valley of Hinnom, south of

Jerusalem. In Jesus's day, Hinnom, or Gehenna, was essentially a city garbage heap where rubbish burned continually and where corpses of executed criminals were dumped. In earlier times, it was where some Israelites engaged in the unthinkable practice of child sacrifice (2 Chronicles 28:3; 33:6). Thus, when Jesus described hell as a place where "the fire never goes out" (Mark 9:44–48 NLT), His listeners could simply glance in the direction of the smoldering "landfill" of Hinnom for a grim illustration.

Another term for hell, borrowed from Greek mythology, means to "cast... into hell" (2 Peter 2:4 ESV).* Peter says this is the destiny of the angels who joined Satan in his rebellion against God. There they are bound in "chains of darkness" and are being "held for judgment."

The Greek word *hades* is synonymous with the Hebrew Old Testament word *sheol*. Rather than a permanent place of punishment, *hades* simply refers to the grave, the temporary realm of the dead, where departed souls await eternal assignment to either heaven or hell.

• • •

Hell—not simply the word but the terrible truth it represents—ought to cause us sleepless nights. The biblical descriptions of a place of unquenchable fire (Matthew 5:22), utter darkness (Matthew 22:13), and ceaseless, restless torment (Revelation 14:10–11) are horrible beyond words.

Even if one regards these images as symbolic or metaphorical, the reality of hell is infinitely worse than we can grasp for this one reason: Hell is the logical destination for those who want nothing to do with God in this life. In the end, they get their wish, separation from Him—forever (2 Thessalonians 1:9).

• • •

---

*This is the word *tartaroo*.

Hell is nothing to joke about or dismiss lightly. Life is short, and eternity is forever. Ask God to break your heart for those who are pushing Him away. Ask Him to soften, open, and transform their hearts.

DISCIPLE

A person who follows a teacher in order to learn
from and become like that teacher

Then Jesus said to his disciples, "Whoever wants to be my disciple must
deny themselves and take up their cross and follow me." (MATTHEW 16:24)

Historians say that Plato was a student of Socrates. George Lucas claims that a long time ago in a galaxy far, far away, Luke Skywalker was tutored by Obi-Wan Kenobi.

More recently actress Elizabeth Taylor was mentored by actress Audrey Hepburn. Almost two millennia before that, Peter, James, Mary Magdalene—and many others—were disciples of Jesus.

• • •

The New Testament Greek word translated *disciple* means "learner" or "student."* In first-century Judaism, discipleship was an arrangement in which a student would literally, physically follow a wise teacher everywhere he went. (Remember, this was before social media and YouTube and online courses.)

The student would tag along, watch and listen attentively, ask and answer questions continually. The goal was to learn and embrace the ideas of the teacher (or rabbi) and to emulate that leader's demeanor and lifestyle.

---

*The Greek word translated "disciple" is *mathetes*.

In Christian circles, then, a disciple is a person who follows Jesus for three reasons: to get to *know* Him and His teaching, to *grow* to be like Him, and to *go* about encouraging others to follow Him.

In these interconnected aspects of knowing, growing, and going, we see that being a disciple of Jesus is all-encompassing. It involves our heads (understanding new truth), our hearts (taking on a new character), and our hands (embarking on a new mission).

• • •

It's fascinating to see how Jesus developed His disciples. Mostly He spent huge amounts of time with them over a three-year period. (No doubt, because truth that comes to us via life events sticks with us more than truth that comes through mere lecture.)

Jesus engaged His students one-on-one, in small group settings, and in big groups. He used sermons, stories, and object lessons. Initially, the disciples did a lot of observing. Over time Jesus began including them more in actual ministry. He gave them ample hands-on training.

At the end of His ministry, as He was preparing to return to heaven, Jesus gathered His students one last time and told them essentially to repeat the process: to go everywhere and show everyone what it looks like to follow Christ (Matthew 28:18–20).

When we read the Gospels, we could summarize Christ's desire for us this way: become disciples who will make disciples.

• • •

The good news about being a follower of Jesus is that the more time we "hang around" Him, the more we become like Him. Consider that when the ordinary Peter stood before the Jewish leaders boldly announcing the resurrection of Jesus, they could tell that He and His friends "had been with Jesus" (Acts 4:13 NLT).

This same kind of transformation is available to us modern-day disciples too.

CROSS

An instrument used by men to take life in the
cruelest possible way—and used by God to give life
in the most amazing way

As they were going out, they met a man from Cyrene, named Simon,
and they forced him to carry the cross. (MATTHEW 27:32)

Exhibited in the Palatine Antiquarium Museum in Rome is a
piece of graffiti discovered by archaeologists in 1857, which
dates back to AD 200. It shows a man with the head of a donkey,
hanging on a cross. To his left another man raises an arm in ado-
ration. The caption reads, "Alexamenos worships his God."

Many scholars consider this drawing the oldest surviving de-
piction of Christ's death. Clearly, it's a mockery of Christianity's
central tenet: that ultimate hope and salvation are found in the
man who was brutally executed on a Roman cross.

• • •

Twenty-seven times in the New Testament we see references
to the cross.[*] The word ought to give us goose bumps.

In the time of Jesus, crosses were used to intimidate, torture,
and execute. A cross was composed of an upright stake in the

---

[*] *Cross* is *stauros* in Greek.

ground, to which a crossbeam was attached, so that the two pieces together resembled the letter T. A person charged with a capital crime would have his arms tied or nailed to the crossbeam, then be lifted up and fastened to the vertical stake.

Crucifixion was a ghastly way to die. Victims were often— as happened with Jesus—flogged first. They hung naked in front of jeering crowds. Breathing was next to impossible. While the sun beat down on them, flies buzzed about them. Death could take days.

The Roman orator Cicero summarized death on the cross this way: "To bind a Roman citizen is a crime, to flog him is an abomination . . . to crucify him is—What? There is no fitting word that can possibly describe so horrible a deed."[*]

•   •   •

Every great story has a moment where the hero runs out of bullets, strength, and options. There's no way out and no way forward. All is lost (or so it seems).

In the great story of God, this moment comes when Jesus, bruised and bloodied almost beyond recognition, hangs limply on a Roman cross.

But then, like a lion, Jesus uses His last bit of energy to cry, "It is finished!" It's a roar, not a whimper, signifying that Jesus has done everything necessary to reverse the great curse that came over the world after the rebellion in Eden. In Christ's unthinkable death, sinners find unimaginable life. The worst Friday ever becomes, oddly, the day we revere as Good Friday.

Paul, obviously realizing how crazy all this sounds, wrote, "For the message of the cross is foolishness to those who are perishing." Then he added, "To us who are being saved it is the power of God" (1 Corinthians 1:18).

---

[*] Cited in John Stott, *The Cross of Christ* (Downers Grove, IL: InterVarsity Press, 1986), 24.

•   •   •

There are some who say it's wrong to turn a terrible instrument of death into a pretty piece of jewelry. But in a way, isn't that what Jesus did? He took the ugliest that humanity had to offer and transformed it into something priceless.

I say wear that cross necklace with joy—and tell others what it really means.

GOSPEL

A good news announcement (in the Bible,
the message of the life, death, and resurrection of Jesus)

And the gospel must first be preached to all nations. (MARK 13:10)

Have you noticed the odd thing that happens when

- someone finds out it's *not* cancer after all;
- a friend's kid hits a desperation shot from half court—
  at the buzzer—to win the championship game;
- sweethearts get engaged;
- empty nesters learn they're going to be grandparents; or
- people win extravagant prizes or prestigious awards?

In these sorts of situations, you almost have to threaten people
to get them to share their good news, right?

What a dumb question!

Good news is impossible *not* to share.

• • •

The New Testament word translated "gospel" (derived from the
Anglo-Saxon word *godspell*) means "good news" or "glad tidings."
In Greek it's *euangelion,* from which we get our English terms
evangelism and *evangelist.*

In ancient times, kings would dispatch heralds to announce the glad tidings of a royal birth or the good news of a victory in battle. In modern times, some companies hire brand evangelists to talk up their products or services.

In a real sense, many of our posts on social media are nothing more than us sharing a gospel—the announcement of a great vacation, a delicious meal, or an accomplishment by one of our kids.

Turns out we're naturally gifted at sharing good news.

• • •

The four gospels of the New Testament are royal announcements from the kingdom of heaven, delivered by the evangelists we know as Matthew, Mark, Luke, and John. They proclaim the birth of a humble but glorious king named Jesus. They chronicle His extraordinary life; His compassion for the broken; His power over sin, disease, nature, evil spirits, and even death itself. They trumpet His sacrificial death for the sinners He loves, and His astonishing victory over the grave. They unashamedly announce His offer of forgiveness and life—new life, eternal life, abundant life—to all who will put their trust in Him.

This good news is the gospel that needs to be announced to all the nations.

• • •

If we're tight-lipped when it comes to talking about who Jesus is and what He has done, the obvious question is, why? We're not mum about any other good news.

Ask God to help you see the gospel of Jesus in a fresh light. Maybe take a few mornings to prayerfully and carefully reread one of the four gospels. As you do, make David's heartfelt prayer—"Restore to me the joy of your salvation" (Psalm 51:12)—your own.

Why is that important? Because we instinctively, automatically talk about things that spark joy in us.

REPENT

To rethink and redirect your life

"The time has come," he said. "The kingdom of God has come near.
Repent and believe the good news!" (MARK 1:15)

For many people (perhaps for you too?) the word *repent* triggers uncomfortable memories: Stern, sweaty preachers thundering away at sin (and at all those sinners squirming in the pews). Deep feelings of spiritual shame. Hot tears of regret. Fears that *maybe God wants to "smite" me?*

• • •

The Old Testament word translated "repent" means "to turn around, go back, or return."* In the New Testament, the Greek word that gets translated "repent" means literally "to change one's mind."†

Putting these two ideas together is a shock to many. Because when they do, they see the biblical idea of repentance is a positive, not a negative, thing! Biblical repentance involves insight from above—having your eyes graciously opened by God's truth—so that you suddenly see in new, true ways. Once you change your

---

*The Hebrew word translated "repent" is *shub*—see 1 Kings 8:47; Psalm 7:12; Jeremiah 5:3.
†The Greek verb translated "repent" is *metanoeo*—see Matthew 3:2; Mark 1:15.

mind about spiritual realities, you can't help but turn back from old, wrong ways. In short, repentance is the act of rethinking and redirecting your life.

Often this life-giving, life-changing insight *does* come through passionate preaching, and it *can* prompt a deeply emotional response. But when it comes to repentance, *feeling badly* takes a backseat to *seeing the truth of God and submitting to it.*

When Jesus officially began His earthly ministry by declaring, "The time has come. . . . The kingdom of God has come near. *Repent* and believe the good news" (Mark 1:15, emphasis added), He wasn't berating anybody. He was saying, "People, open your eyes! See what's true! Then come back! Come home! Put your faith in me and believe the good news I'm announcing."

• • •

In short, the biblical call to repent, to turn *away* from sin and return *to* God, is less a condemnation and more an invitation! The Lord is trying to steer us away from paths that, though they look appealing, actually lead to great harm (Proverbs 14:12). His desire is for us to find life in all its fullness (John 10:10).

Martin Luther said, "When our Lord and Master Jesus Christ said, 'Repent,' he willed the entire life of believers to be one of repentance."* In other words, repentance is not a one-time act at the beginning of the spiritual life; it's an ongoing, daily practice for believers. It's as we continually study God's Word, and follow the promptings of God's Spirit, that our minds are renewed and our lives are transformed (Romans 12:2).

---

*This is the first of Luther's famous *Ninety-Five Theses*, a document posted on the church door in Wittenberg, Germany, on October 31, 1517 (and the document that ignited the Protestant Reformation).

• • •

Obviously, it's not enough to simply know the meaning of the word *repent*. Disciples are people who consistently live as Jesus commands (John 14:21)—people who "do the word" (James 1:22).

In what specific part of your life today do you need new insight—and to go in a different direction? Ask God to show you what repentance looks like . . .

in your work life,

in your family interactions,

in how you view and handle money,

in an unresolved conflict,

in how you engage those who are far from God,

in how you spend your time,

in your use of social media,

in your attitudes toward others.

CHRIST

The Anointed One of God who is the true Savior and King

For unto you is born this day in the city of David a Savior,
who is Christ the Lord. (LUKE 2:11 ESV)

The story never gets old, no matter how many times we hear it each Christmas.

Some shepherds keeping a sleepy eye on a snoozing flock. A night that probably *was* silent—at least until it was shattered by an explosion of divine glory.

An angelic announcement from on high. A message too good to be true, or too good not to be true—*Christ was born today in Bethlehem*—followed by a few instructions on how to find Him and a heavenly flash mob appearing out of nowhere to praise God.

Awestruck shepherds dashing—likely through mud, not snow—to Bethlehem to gawk at a newborn Jewish boy lying in a makeshift crib.

● ● ●

Christ—which is a title, not a surname—is the Greek translation of the Hebrew word *Messiah* (*mashiach*). *Messiah* means "anointed one" and comes from the verb *masach*, which was used to describe the Jewish ritual of pouring oil on the head of a God-appointed prophet (1 Kings 19:16), priest (Exodus 29:7), or king (2 Samuel 12:7).

Over the years, many of those anointed servants of God—prophets like Isaiah and kings like David—wrote of a coming day when the Lord would finally anoint Israel's greatest Prophet, Priest, and King (John 1:41)—all rolled into one! He would be the Savior Israel had spent centuries praying and waiting for.

It's staggering to think that when Christ finally came, the first people alerted were some lowly shepherds camped in a nearby field. Of course, who better to welcome "the Lamb of God, who takes away the sin of the world" (John 1:29) than a group of shepherds?

• • •

Most Bible teachers point to the baptism of Jesus (Matthew 3:16–17)—some thirty years after His birth (Luke 3:23)—as His anointing. There the Spirit descended on Him like a dove and a voice from heaven declared this Nazarene carpenter-turned-rabbi "my Son, whom I love" (Matthew 3:17).

With that, this Savior-King we know as Jesus Christ officially began His ministry of seeking and saving the lost (Luke 19:10).

• • •

The Gospels record an incident in which Jesus surveyed His disciples, "Who do people say I am?" (Mark 8:27). After they shared some of the things they'd been hearing on the old grapevine, Jesus changed the question, "But what about you? . . . Who do you say I am?" (v. 29). Peter shot back, "You are the Messiah" (v. 29). Jesus blessed Peter for giving the correct answer (Matthew 16:17)—and later gave it himself to some people who didn't exactly share Peter's fervent belief (Matthew 26:63–64).

It comes down to that question: Who do we say Jesus is? Do we believe He is the Christ, the Son of the living God (Matthew 16:16)?

BAPTIZE

A meaningful New Testament ritual that pictures
acceptance into God's family of faith

I baptize you with water. But one who is more powerful than I will . . .
baptize you with the Holy Spirit and fire. (LUKE 3:16)

Some people are shocked to discover the Bible never actually
says, "Cleanliness is next to godliness."

What the story of God shows instead is various ritual wash-
ings in the Old Testament (Exodus 30:17–21; Leviticus 16:3–4)
and something called "baptism" in the New Testament.

• • •

The first three gospels (Matthew 3:1–17; Mark 1:2–11; Luke 3:1–
20) begin with a flurry of baptisms. Specifically, a man named
John appears in the wilderness southeast of Jerusalem and thunders, "Repent!" to all who will listen.

Soon people are flocking from Jerusalem to hear this insect-
eating prophet, who dresses like Elijah. And they don't just listen to
him, they line up in front of him. Matthew tells us, "Confessing
their sins, they were baptized by him in the Jordan River" (3:6).

Our English verb *baptized* comes straight from the Greek *bap-
tizo*. It means "to dip" or "immerse." Can you see it? People wading

into the Jordan—either to disappear under the water, or to have water sprinkled or poured over them. This ceremony was anticipatory. It looked forward to the day when one greater than John— that is, Jesus—would also baptize His followers, not with mere H_2O (Mark 1:8) but with the Holy Spirit of God!

Following his death and resurrection, Jesus gave His disciples the command to go and take His message everywhere. Part of that job description? Baptizing every new believer.

• • •

Like so many spiritual activities—prayer, communion, confession, and so on—baptism is understood and practiced in many different ways.

Here's what we can agree on: Religious rituals are powerless to make anyone right with God. It is faith alone in Christ alone that saves us (John 3:16; Ephesians 2:8–9).

We could liken getting baptized to putting on a wedding ring. Wearing jewelry doesn't make a person married (*that* requires making vows and signing a marriage license in the presence of witnesses). A ring is simply a visible expression of an invisible reality. Baptism is like that—an outward symbol of an inward commitment to Jesus Christ.

Baptism serves as a powerful illustration of some important spiritual realities: (a) the death and burial of one's old life; (b) immersion into the life of Christ—and union with Him; (c) cleansing from sin; and (d) resurrection with Jesus into a brand-new life.

Baptism further functions as a kind of initiation. It's a way for the church to say, "Welcome to the forever family of God!"

• • •

The book of Acts shows people being baptized soon after placing their faith in Christ (Acts 2:41; 8:38–39; 10:47–48). Maybe this is your experience as well. Or maybe you were raised in a faith tradition that observes infant baptism.

If you're a believer in Christ, but you've never been baptized, here's something to consider. Baptism is a great way to go public with your faith. In addition to being an illustration and an initiation, it's also a proclamation. It says to others, I want to be identified by others as a follower of Jesus.

LOST

To be in the wrong place or in a perilous state
or a ruined condition

For the Son of Man came to seek and to save the lost. (LUKE 19:10)

The same week your parents lost a big chunk of their retirement money in a bad investment, a coworker lost everything in a fire. Last month, your teenager lost track of time and consequently lost her job. Last year, your brother temporarily lost his way with the result that he lost his marriage. A dear friend lost a brave battle with cancer, meaning you lost part of your heart.

Unless we're talking about losing unwanted pounds, there aren't many four-letter words as foul as *lost*.

● ● ●

Six times in the gospel of Luke, Jesus speaks of lost things. And He doesn't just mean they've been misplaced. The word conveys the idea of something valuable that isn't where or what it was meant to be.* Take the three well-known parables Jesus told in Luke 15. The lost sheep is somewhere "out there" wandering, in danger of being devoured. The lost coin is of no use to its owner. It's wasted. The lost son who hightailed it to a far country to

---

*The New Testament Greek word for *lost* is *apollymi*.

engage in riotous living is headed for destruction. That's not all: the other, older son who stayed home is equally lost—lost in bitterness and envy. He's also lost the capacity to feel compassion.

To be lost, in the biblical sense, is be trapped in a kind of "living death." You no longer know why you're here, what you're doing, or where you're going. You're not what you were meant to be. You certainly aren't what you could be.

• • •

The good news Jesus announces is that He is the seeker and the Savior of lost causes. He's the shepherd who searches high and low for the missing sheep. He's the intense woman who turns her house upside down in search of the precious coin. He's the father who stands at the end of the driveway, scanning the horizon for the foolish boy. And when the old man spots him far off, red-faced, hands jammed in his pockets, he takes off running. What follows is the mother of all bear hugs. Tears of joy. The fattened calf. A party for the ages.

• • •

There's *Lost* (with a capital L), and then there's *lost*. The former is the ultimate kind of ruin—being separated from God and missing the life He longs to give you. The latter is a temporary condition. You look up to see you've strayed. You're off the path and in the weeds. *How did I end up here?*

Whatever form of lostness you're experiencing—whether it's your very soul that's lost, or your job or your joy—Jesus is the one you need. And the good news is you don't have to go off on a long search for Him. If you call Him, He'll come right to where you are. He'll find you.

BELIEVE

To trust in a person or a claim one considers credible

Then Jesus told him, "Go back home. Your son will live!" And the man
believed what Jesus said and started home. (JOHN 4:50 NLT)

A man's got to believe in something," says a character in a Peter
DeVries novel, before pausing and adding, "I believe I'll have
another drink."

We might question the man's choices, but there's no denying
his point. Humans *have* to believe. Not believing is not possible.

Everybody lives by faith, all day every day. Faith that our very
existence is real and not an elaborate hallucination. Faith that certain actions will produce certain results. Faith that the brownies
left in the break room are full of deliciousness—and not some
deadly toxin.

That we all believe is undeniable. Figuring out *what* we believe is where things get interesting.

• • •

In the fourth gospel, John was obsessed with the idea of belief;
in fact, he used forms of the verb *believe* almost a hundred times!

The word conveys the idea of trusting in something (or someone) you regard as trustworthy.* You believe because, well, a person or claim strikes you as believable.

John is honest about why he wrote his account of the life of Jesus. After relating certain teachings of Jesus and selected miracles, John concludes, "Jesus performed many other signs in the presence of his disciples, which are not recorded in this book. But these are written that you may believe that Jesus is the Messiah, the Son of God, and that by believing you may have life in his name" (John 20:30–31).

John was saying that of all the things we could choose to believe in this crazy world, he wanted us to trust that Jesus is the God-sent Savior of the world. John was convinced the life we need is found only in Jesus. He wants us to believe that too.

● ● ●

Skeptics argue that believing in Jesus is like believing in the tooth fairy or Sasquatch, or believing that Captain Marvel is real. The Creator entering His own creation? The Almighty working as a carpenter in first-century Israel, then being executed and rising from the dead? John is essentially saying, "It might sound far-fetched, but I was there. I saw what I saw. I know what I know. I'm asking you to trust my testimony. More than that, I'm pleading with you to put your faith in the One I'm telling you about."

● ● ●

The tricky thing about believing is that it takes faith. That's not meant to be a wisecrack. Rather, it's a recognition that it always comes down to trust. Ultimately, we have to regard someone's word or research as credible, then put our confidence in their character.

---

* *Believe* is *pisteuo* in Greek.

Some days, believing the claims of the Christian faith comes easily. Other days, our hearts fill with questions and what-ifs, and believing is like storming the beach at Iwo Jima.

Maybe this is why in John 15:5, John records Jesus's statement, "Apart from me you can do nothing."

Such a sweeping statement would seem to mean we can't even believe without help from above.

Having trouble believing? Ask the Lord for the grace to trust His words (see Mark 9:24).

LIFE

Physical—and in the Bible, spiritual—vitality,
not possessed by that which is dead or inorganic

The thief comes only to steal and kill and destroy; I have come that they
may have life, and have it to the full. (John 10:10)

Early in our tour of important (but misunderstood and under-appreciated) Bible words, we paused to ponder the word *die* (chapter 3). We saw there the logical consequence of spurning the One who *is* life itself, the One who *gives* life: a world full of mortuaries and obituaries, graveyards and grief counselors. We saw too the horrifying spiritual consequences: alienation from the living God, consignment to a kind of "living death."

Thankfully, God wasn't—and isn't—okay with any of that.

• • •

Most mentions of life in the New Testament employ the Greek word *zōē*. This word can simply refer to the miracle of natural, earthly, everyday life—breathing, thinking, eating an omelet, fetching a Frisbee off the roof.* Jesus, however, typically focused

---

*To be clear, the Bible doesn't mention omelets or Frisbees. These are simply modern-day examples of what physical life (*zōē*) looks like.

on an even more miraculous kind of life—the new, spiritual, supernatural, endless life He came to offer.

Again and again Jesus promised eternal life to those who would trust Him (John 3:16, 36; 5:24; 6:47). He defined that eternal life as knowing God personally and entering into a relationship with Him (John 17:3). He lamented those who "refuse to come to me to have life" (John 5:40).

Jesus described himself as "the bread of life" who "gives life to the world" (John 6:33, 48). He called himself "the resurrection and the life" (John 11:25) and, simply, "the life" (John 14:6). To confirm these extravagant claims, on at least three occasions, Jesus brought dead people back from the grave. No wonder His followers called Him "the author of life" (Acts 3:15)!

• • •

In John 10:10, Jesus described the life He offers His sheep (i.e., His followers) as "life . . . to the full." It's a statement worth contemplating. The adjective *full* means "extraordinary, more than normal, overflowing, superabundant." In some contexts, it suggests an amount almost too much to bear.

• • •

Here are some questions about life to wrestle with:

- Who is the most "alive" person I know?
- Am I living the kind of "full" life Jesus described in John 10:10? If not, what's keeping me from enjoying this kind of rich life (and who can I trust to help me process this question)?
- What in my life seems to be on life support—or maybe even dead?

- What if I invited the risen Christ to live in and through me today? What if I allowed His Spirit to animate me and empower me right now? What remarkable things might I see?

ABIDE

To dwell in a place long-term

Abide in me, and I in you. As the branch cannot bear fruit by itself, unless it abides in the vine, neither can you, unless you abide in me. (JOHN 15:4 ESV)

Consider these findings:

- The average American moves to a new home 11.4 times over a lifetime.[*]
- The average worker changes jobs about twelve times during his or her career.[†]
- The average person stays on a webpage less than one minute before leaving.[‡]

Clearly, we are a restless race. Staying put is not our strong suit. Which may be why the Bible makes such a fuss over the word *abide*.

● ● ●

---

[*] Mona Chalabi, "How Many Times Does the Average Person Move?" FiveThirtyEight, January 29, 2015, https://fivethirtyeight.com/features/how-many-times-the-average-person-moves/. (This figure is much lower for Europeans.)

[†] Alison Doyle, "How Often Do People Change Jobs," www.thebalancecareers.com, last modified January 2, 2020, https://www.thebalancecareers.com/how-often-do-people-change-careers-3969407.

[‡] Jakob Nielson, "How Long Do Users Stay on Web Pages?" www.nngroup, last modified September 11, 2011, https://www.nngroup.com/articles/how-long-do-users-stay-on-web-pages/.

Ten times in John 15:4–11, we find the verb *abide* on the lips of Jesus, and what a rich term it is.* It conveys the idea of remaining in a place. *Staying* there. *Dwelling* there. *Abide* isn't a motel stay; it's a mortgage. You're not an overnight guest. You unpack, kick off your shoes, and settle in for the long haul.

This is why people sometimes receive visitors into their homes with the statement, "Welcome to our humble abode." An abode is where one abides or lives. Jesus communicated this idea in John 14:23 when He promised, "Anyone who loves me will obey my teaching. My Father will love them, and we will come to them and *make our home with* them" (emphasis added).

• • •

Don't forget . . . even as Jesus was hammering away at this idea of abiding, He knew Roman soldiers would be hammering Him to a cross in less than twenty-four hours! It was no time for small talk. He used the analogy of a vine and branches to illustrate that abiding means intimate connection and deep attachment.

Abide in me, and let me abide in you, Jesus said (15:4). If you do, you'll experience a fruitful life that honors God and blesses others (15:5). Let my words abide you, He urged (15:7). When you do, you'll see amazing answers to prayer. Abide in my love, He said. How? By keeping my commands (15:9–10).

• • •

Abide is not a word that—ahem—abides in the daily vocabularies of most of us. It feels a little archaic. But whether we use the word or not, the practice of abiding is life-changing.

If you'd like to know more about establishing and maintaining this kind of constant connection with the Lord, find a copy

---

* *Meno* is the Greek verb translated variously as "to abide," "to remain," or "to stay."

of the 300-year-old classic by Brother Lawrence called *The Practice of the Presence of God.* This simple book by a humble friar explains the vanishing art of abiding.

SPIRIT

The divine Person responsible for spiritual life, growth, and service

But you will receive power when the Holy Spirit comes on you;
and you will be my witnesses in Jerusalem, and in all Judea and Samaria,
and to the ends of the earth. (Acts 1:8)

From beginning (Genesis 1:2) to end (Revelation 22:17), the great story of God is sprinkled with references to the Spirit. We read about the "Spirit of God" (Exodus 31:3), the "Spirit of the Lord" (Isaiah 40:13; Ezekiel 11:5), the "Spirit of truth" (John 14:17; 16:13), and the "Holy Spirit" (Psalm 51:11; Acts 1:8). (Older translations of the Bible refer to the "Holy Ghost.")

What do we make of all these Spirit references?

• • •

The literal meaning of the biblical word *spirit* is "wind or breath."*

This is interesting because we can't see wind—only the effects of it. And unless we're outside on a cold day, we can't see our breath either. So to speak of God as Spirit (John 4:24) is to say that He is by nature invisible.

---

*The Hebrew word translated "spirit" is *ruah.* The New Testament equivalent is the Greek word *pneuma.*

Another consideration: life utterly depends on breath. The person who stops breathing will soon die—unless another person blows air into her lungs or a machine starts breathing for him. Thus, to speak of God as Spirit is to say that He's the breath of humanity (Job 12:10; Isaiah 42:5). He is the giver and sustainer of life.

•　•　•

The astonishing claim of Christianity is that there once was a man who temporarily made the invisible God visible (John 1:1, 14; 14:9; Colossians 1:15–16). In Jesus, the infinite Creator came and rubbed shoulders (literally) with His finite creatures.

Then, just before He left, Jesus made a shocking promise to His followers: that He would soon send them "another advocate"—one just like himself, only invisible—to live inside them forever (John 14:16–17). He called this promised one the Holy Spirit (Acts 1:8).

Talk about a divine breath! In Acts 2, the Spirit swept powerfully over and through the people of God, a life-giving hurricane of hope and help! The result was God's new community: the church.

•　•　•

The New Testament frequently discusses the Spirit of God—and we're wise to review those truths often. Consider these teachings:

- The Spirit is fully God—in the same way Jesus is (Acts 5:1–4).
- Jesus constantly referred to the Spirit as "He"—meaning we should stop calling Him an "it." God's Spirit is a divine Person, not some vague, heavenly energy.
- The Spirit lives within the heart of every believer (Romans 8:9, 11).

- The Spirit prays nonstop for all of us (Romans 8:26–27).
- The Spirit gives Christians supernatural abilities for serving others (Romans 12:3–8).

As the "Holy" Spirit, he's constantly leading us toward truth and away from error and unholiness (John 16:13). He elbows us in the soul when we start to stray (John 16:7–8), and He's grieved when we ignore His promptings (Ephesians 4:30). Why? Because His primary goal is to make us like Christ (Galatians 4:19; 5:22–23).

Feeling suffocated—like your soul can't *breathe*? Feeling spent—like you need a powerful, second *wind*?

God's Spirit can fill you with new vitality and power. Just ask Him.

CHURCH

Believers in Christ (locally and globally)
who share a common life in Christ

They gathered the church together and reported all that God had done
through them and how he had opened a door of faith to the Gentiles.
(Acts 14:27)

Here's an important Bible word that makes more people groan
than grin:

Church.

Bet you have some stories you could tell. (Don't we all?)

What are we to make of this entity with a long history of helping—and hurting? How can a congregation of Christians be such
a mess one day and such a masterpiece the next?

• • •

Ekklesia is the Greek word translated "church" more than one
hundred times in the New Testament. Literally referring to those
who have been "called out," this word usually conveys a local assembly of believers in Christ (think church, lowercase *c*). In other
passages, *ekklesia* refers to all believers everywhere (think Church,
capital *c*). Either way, *church* always means people, an assembly
or gathering of souls. It's not a building where religious services
are held.

Most people agree that the church began when the Holy Spirit was poured out on the first-century Jewish followers of Jesus in Jerusalem (see Acts 2). From that point on, as the apostles set out to follow Jesus's command to make disciples of all nations (Matthew 28:18–19), more and more people—Jews and Gentiles—put their faith in Christ. As they began following Him together in various locales, local congregations began to spring up.

● ● ●

If the church is people (and it is), then voila! There's our answer for why church is such a mixed bag—encouraging in some ways and discouraging in others. Those who make up the church—including those in leadership—are flawed and flaky. This is because salvation doesn't immediately perfect believers—it merely starts a lifelong construction project within us! Therefore, church people have good moments and bad ones. Sometimes we see the needs of others and rush in to help. Other times we're so wrapped up in our own problems or pain, we're oblivious to those around us.

A beautiful description of the early church is found in Acts 2:42–47. There we see believers who "devoted themselves to . . . fellowship." *Fellowship* refers to what we share, what we have in common.*

The fact is, we have much in common (even when we *seem* very different). A common problem: sin. A common need: salvation. A common Savior: Jesus. A common life: new life in Christ. A common calling: to follow Jesus. A common mission: to help others follow Jesus.

● ● ●

When churches do goofy things or Christians act in hypocritical ways, it's tempting to want to distance yourself from the body

---

*Fellowship is an English translation of the Greek term *koinonia*; it is sometimes rendered *community.*

of Christ. Don't! Find a group of believers to do life with and plug in. Bring your authentic self—the good, the bad, and the ugly.

You *need* a group like that. And believe it or not, they need you. Not gonna lie: you'll occasionally drive each other nuts. You'll also help each other make it home.

APOSTLES

Eyewitnesses of Christ who were sent by Him
to share the good news and lead the church

With great power the apostles continued to testify to the resurrection of
the Lord Jesus. And God's grace was so powerfully at work in them all.

(ACTS 4:33)

In the Old Testament, the Lord sent prophets. In the New Testament, He sent apostles.

Matthew gives us a list of the men handpicked by Jesus: "These are the names of the twelve apostles: first, Simon (who is called Peter) and his brother Andrew; James son of Zebedee, and his brother John; Philip and Bartholomew; Thomas and Matthew the tax collector; James son of Alphaeus, and Thaddaeus; Simon the Zealot and Judas Iscariot, who betrayed him" (Matthew 10:2–4).

According to Mark's gospel, an apostle's job description had two parts: being with Jesus and being sent out to preach by Jesus (3:14).

• • •

"One who is sent out on behalf of another"—*that* is the literal and technical meaning of the word *apostle*. The idea is that of a messenger, envoy, or emissary. From the church's beginning in Acts 2, the apostles of Jesus preached that He was (and is) the Christ—God's Son, Israel's Messiah and King, the world's Savior.

The apostles broadcast the truth of Christ's resurrection. They passed on His teachings (Acts 2:42). They performed the same kinds of eye-opening miracles that Jesus had done (Acts 2:43; 5:12). Like Christ, they were persecuted by government officials and religious leaders (Acts 5:40–41), with at least one, James, being martyred before Luke even finished the book of Acts (see Acts 12:1–3). Together with Paul (Acts 9), a late addition to their number, the apostles wrote, or in a few cases supervised, the writing of the New Testament documents.

● ● ●

When we think about the character of Jesus and the mission of Jesus, we can't help feeling shocked at the apostles Jesus chose to represent him. They weren't exactly a lineup of all-stars. Often prideful, self-centered, skeptical, judgmental, and unreliable, none of the original twelve had formal biblical or theological training. At the most critical moment, they all left Jesus high and dry.

Yet because of Christ's fierce love, they were forgiven. And through His resurrection power, they were transformed.

● ● ●

He sent them out (Matthew 28:18–20). They went. The world has never been the same.

We don't get to be Apostles (capital *A*). Qualifying for that elite role required being an eyewitness of Jesus's resurrection.

We can, however, be apostles (lowercase *a*). In the spirit of Mark 3:14, every believer can be "with Jesus" and be sent out by Him to declare the good news.

Maybe at the start of each day we could co-opt the prophet Isaiah's prayer: "Here I am. Send me" (Isaiah 6:8 NLT).

PAUL

A native of Tarsus chosen by Jesus to be an
apostle and missionary; writer of at least thirteen
New Testament epistles

Then some Jews came from Antioch and Iconium and won the crowd over.
They stoned Paul and dragged him outside the city, thinking he was dead.
But after the disciples had gathered around him, he got up and went back into
the city. The next day he and Barnabas left for Derbe. (ACTS 14:19–20)

An ancient tradition suggests Paul was a short, balding man with a unibrow and a hooked nose. God only knows if that's accurate. What we can say for sure is that this bulldog of a man was (and is) the poster child for God's grace.

Consider these stunning realities:

- While stalking Christians, Paul was stalked by Christ himself (Acts 9:1–5)!
- While in the act of persecuting Jesus (Acts 9:5), Paul was chosen for a new life of preaching Jesus (Acts 9:15)!
- In a flash (literally), Paul went from "breathing out murderous threats against the Lord's disciples" (Acts 9:1) to trying "to join the disciples" (Acts 9:26)!

• • •

The name Paul means "small," and never was there a more ill-fitting name. After being confronted and converted by the risen Christ on the road to Damascus, Paul (known by his Hebrew name Saul at the time) retreated to Arabia for an extended time of study and reflection (Galatians 1:17). After that, this ancient, apostolic "Energizer Bunny" got busy, tirelessly taking the gospel into Asia Minor, then Europe. In the synagogues of the cities he visited, he always made an effort to reach out to his fellow Jews. In secular settings, he shared Christ's love with every Gentile who would listen.

In most locales, Paul was the catalyst for either a revival or a riot—sometimes both. Occasionally he was forced to flee for his life; other times he was allowed to unpack his bags for long stretches and teach the ways of God. On the missionary journeys recorded in the book of Acts, Paul planted churches the way the Arbor Society plants trees. Before, after, and during these trips, he wrote letters (to both individuals and congregations) that unpack the gospel and its implications for people living in a hostile world.

Small Paul? Nice try. The man was and is a colossus of the Christian faith.

• • •

Paul's life is a vivid picture of God's grace. He wasn't hungering to know Jesus. In fact, Paul was driven by religious rage *against* Jesus (not too far removed from the radicals we read about today who try to blow up those who don't believe as they do).

This is why his sudden, unexpected conversion gives us hope. If Jesus can save a person like Paul, whom won't He save?

• • •

If you've never done so (or haven't done so in a while), read the New Testament writings about Paul and by Paul. Acts (chapters 9, 13–28) tells the story of how he met Christ and what followed. And the epistles of Paul (Romans through Philemon) discuss the ramifications of the gospel for everyday life. They're incredibly deep and wonderfully practical. They'll bother you and comfort you. They'll make you think and make you thankful.

SIN

Rejecting God and His rule—
and thus rebelling against His will

For the wages of sin is death, but the gift of God is eternal life
in Christ Jesus our Lord. (ROMANS 6:23)

Humanity's biggest crisis isn't climate change or the threat of nuclear war. (And—apologies to any sci-fi fans who happen to be reading—it's not robots taking over either.) The biggest emergency facing the human race isn't poverty or pollution—or the threat of some pandemic.

According to the Bible, those terrible evils and ills are only symptoms of a deeper, more pervasive problem: the deadly virus in the human soul called *sin*.

• • •

The word translated "sin" in the verse above means "to miss the mark."* Picture an archer failing to hit the bull's-eye. At first blush, that doesn't seem so bad—at least he was trying, right?

It's when we read the detailed, biblical descriptions of *sin* that we get a more complete—and more sickening—picture. Sinning is rebelling (see chapter 12) and going astray (Isaiah 53:6). It's

---

*The Greek term for *sin* here is *hamartia*.

SIN

transgressing (that is, willfully crossing lines we know we shouldn't cross). Lest anyone miss the point, the Bible keeps piling up the ugly adjectives. Sin is wickedness, hypocrisy, ungodliness, lawlessness, and unrighteousness. And the kicker? We're all guilty—every single one of us (Romans 3:23)—whether we *feel* guilty or not.

Miss the mark? Of course we missed it! That's because most days, we weren't even trying to hit it, weren't even *thinking* about the mark.

● ● ●

In short, the New Testament says we do sinful things because we have a sinful nature. That's the crux of the issue. Sin is the hardened stance of every son of Adam and daughter of Eve against God and His authority. The bad news? The "wages of sin"—that is, what sin earns us—is death. The good news of the gospel? Through Jesus, God offers sinful people eternal life.

When we trust in Christ, the living God forgives our sin and makes our dead souls come alive. (How's that for a divine mic drop?)

● ● ●

As we keep reading in Romans, what we discover is that God doesn't merely rescue us from the penalty of sin—as marvelous as that is. He also promises us power to overcome the pull of sin.

Read Romans 5–8. Since faith *in* Christ means union *with* Christ, we're dead now to old ways of living. We've "been set free from sin" (Romans 6:7) and now have resurrection power to "live a new life" (Romans 6:4).

Grappling with those truths—and helping others grasp them—won't change the world overnight. But, hey, it's a really good start.

77

GRACE

Getting blessing when we least deserve it

The God of peace will soon crush Satan under your feet.
The grace of our Lord Jesus be with you. (ROMANS 16:20)

Even in our graceless culture, we still sometimes encounter the word *grace*. A God-fearing aunt offers to "say grace" over a meal. The fine print on a credit card statement mentions a "grace period." A news story tells of a popular celebrity's "stunning fall from grace."

Of all the dazzling words in the Bible, *grace* might be the most beautiful—which is saying a mouthful. It is also one of the hardest to grasp.

• • •

Grace means "unmerited favor." It's the idea of getting blessings we don't deserve.*

As such, grace is mind-bending. It's *not* the way of the world. When bad people do bad things, we don't want our judges doling out grace. We want them throwing the book at thugs and lowlifes. (Hey, if we had the chance, we'd throw some things too, at least a few choice words!) This is why the Eastern notion of karma is so popular in Western culture—the thought of guilty people getting

---

* *Grace* is *hēn* in the Old Testament, *charis* in the New Testament.

just what they deserve makes us stand up and cheer—at least until we remember our own sin (see previous chapter). The inconvenient truth that we're each guilty of treason against the King of the universe and deserving of the ultimate punishment? Big problem!

Except that God "does not treat us as our sins deserve" (Psalm 103:10)! He governs by grace not karma! In history's most shocking switcheroo, God took our sin and the harsh judgment it deserves and laid all that on Jesus. Then to undeserving sinners who put their trust in Jesus, He gives unimaginable blessing!

Karma says, "You deserve to pay." Grace says, "It's true—you do deserve to pay; however, since Jesus took the punishment you deserve, by faith you can have all the good things He deserves."

(Before you ponder that too deeply, you might want to grab the smelling salts.)

• • •

The apostle Paul not only ended Romans by wishing his readers grace (16:20), he began the letter with a similar benediction (1:7). Alert readers note that he did this frequently in his New Testament letters.

The most likely reason for this endearing habit? Since the grace of God was easily the best gift Paul ever received, it was the one blessing he wanted most for everyone else.

• • •

Definitions can't affect our hearts like stories can, so read two of the great stories of grace from the Bible. Start with the story of the lost sons in Luke 15:11–32. Then check out the moving, mind-boggling story of Manasseh (2 Chronicles 33:1–20).

To quote an old West Texas cowboy, "If those stories don't ring your bell, your clapper's broke."

78

RESURRECTION

The act of raising the dead to life
(physically and in every other way)

For since death came through a man, the resurrection of the dead
comes also through a man. (1 CORINTHIANS 15:21)

Growing numbers of people, facing the grim reality of mortality, are turning to science (or maybe science fiction). Believing that researchers are close to figuring out how to eliminate disease, reverse the effects of aging, and eradicate death, some are forking over big bucks to have their bodies placed, immediately upon death, in "cryonic suspension." (This is sciencespeak for "being stored in liquid nitrogen, a substance so cold it would give the North Pole a serious case of frostbite.") Their hope is that if scientists discover the secret to immortality, their frozen bodies can be reanimated or resuscitated.

The Bible offers a better, surer hope for those facing death: resurrection.

• • •

Stories of certifiably dead people being brought back to life are found throughout the story of God. The Old Testament prophets Elijah (1 Kings 17:8–24) and Elisha (2 Kings 4:18–37) performed such miracles. In the New Testament, Jesus (Mark 5:35–43; Luke 7:11–17; John 11:17–44), Peter (Acts 9:36–42), and Paul

(Acts 20:9–12) also raised people from the dead. In one sense, however, these resurrections feel incomplete—so far as we can tell, they were only temporary reprieves from death.

The resurrection* of Jesus was different. It was permanent (Romans 6:9). And in 1 Corinthians 15, Paul talked about how Christ's conquering of the grave was a kind of preview of coming attractions (vv. 22–23). It signaled the glorious fact that all those in Christ will one day experience everything He did—the remaking of our old, perishable, flawed, weak physical bodies into new, imperishable, glorious, powerful, spiritual bodies.

● ● ●

In the earliest days of the church, the bodily resurrection of Jesus was central to the apostles' preaching. Paul said it was essential to the Christian faith, telling the believers in Corinth, "if Christ has not been raised, your faith is futile; you are still in your sins" (1 Corinthians 15:17).

The resurrection is also crucial for another reason. The fact that Jesus had a touchable body means that eternity for us won't be a matter of floating through the heavens like disembodied ghosts in the ether. We'll be fully alive in the new heaven and new earth, completely redeemed souls in totally restored bodies.

No liquid nitrogen needed.

● ● ●

Finally, at the most practical level, the biblical truth of resurrection means God is powerful enough to make dead things live again—with a vitality not seen before.

What in your life could use God's resurrecting touch? A marriage? Your church? Your passion for your work? A friendship

---

* *Resurrection* is the English translation of the Greek word *anastasis*.

or relationship with a child? Why not express to the Father the same thing Paul said: "I want to know Christ—yes, to know the power of his resurrection" (Philippians 3:10)?

SAINT

One who has been chosen by God
and set apart for His holy purposes

Paul, an apostle of Christ Jesus by the will of God, and Timothy our
brother, to the church of God which is at Corinth with all the saints who
are throughout Achaia . . . (2 Corinthians 1:1 nasb)

Ask people "What's a saint?" and most will answer something like, "An extremely devoted Christian." Protestants think of the apostles—referred to in older versions of the Bible as St. Peter, St. Paul, St. Matthew, and so on. Catholics have a much longer list of holy men and women venerated through church history. Catholic saints include the familiar names of missionaries like St. Patrick, St. Francis, or St. Teresa (formerly Mother Teresa).

One common assumption from all this "saint talk" is that Christ's church is made up of two distinct classes of Christians: hordes of bumbling, stumbling, nothing-special believers; and a small, rare group of spiritual superstars.

Is that true? In Christ's kingdom, are everyday Christians the common house cats and saints the exotic snow leopards?

• • •

Almost seventy times, the New Testament writers refer to everyday believers as "saints," translated in some Bible versions as "holy people" (NIV, NLT).* The word comes from the same New Testament root that gets translated "sanctify," "sanctification," or "holy."

If that's clear as mud, just know this: *sanctify* means "to set apart." The first time we see this word in the Bible is all the way back in Genesis 2:3 when God *sanctified* the Sabbath day. That is, He separated it from the other six days. He deemed it special and not for common use (that's the basic idea of holiness).

The Bible says that sanctification—not sure why we don't just call it saint-ification—is both a moment-in-time event and a life-long process. God regards us as holy, as saints, the moment we believe in Jesus (1 Corinthians 6:11)—then He helps us become progressively more holy, or saintly, as we love and serve Him (1 Peter 1:15).

• • •

This means if you're a believer in Jesus, in God's eyes, you *are* a saint. Right now! And *sainthood* means at least three amazing things are true. First, you have a new nature (2 Corinthians 5:17). Your new identity is no longer "sinner." Will you still sin? Of course! But those failures don't make you a sinner. They make you a saint who sometimes screws up. Second, you're also under new ownership. God has made you His own. Third, you have a new purpose. God has reserved you for His holy and amazing purposes.

• • •

Take the biblical teaching of sainthood to heart. Believe what God says about you. Whenever we forget our God-given identity, sin seems reasonable and logical. But when we embrace the biblical claim that God has made and is making us holy, we see sin for what it truly is: foolish and irrational.

*The word *saints* is *hagios* in Greek.

One last thing: Because you are a saint, the desire to do right and to please God is always within you. You may not always *sense* that; that may not always *feel* true, but it *is* true. It has to be. In Christ, you're a new creature with a new nature. You're a living, breathing saint.

FREEDOM

Liberation from bondage to someone or something

For you have been called to live in freedom, my brothers and sisters.
But don't use your freedom to satisfy your sinful nature. Instead, use your
freedom to serve one another in love. (GALATIANS 5:13 NLT)

For *free* people in a *free* society, it sure does seem like a lot of folks are trapped in miserable ways of living.

Some human hang-ups are easy to see—the off-the-charts workaholic. The nephew who's hoping a fourth attempt at rehab will work. The angry boss everyone calls Old Faithful—because of how routinely she erupts.

Often, however, it's *not* easy to tell what's controlling people. Maybe it's chronic anxiety or a secret addiction to pornography. Maybe it's an overwhelming compulsion to please others. How many are at the mercy of pride or perfectionism, envy, guilt, or shame? And what about the millions who've been captured by the lie that following religious rules will earn them God's approval?

Paul wrote the New Testament letter of Galatians to help people like that—like *us*—find freedom.

• • •

Freedom in the Bible often refers to physical release from captivity or imprisonment (Mark 15:6; Acts 16:35)—even deliverance from illness (Luke 13:12).

Paul, however, uses the beautiful Greek word *eleutheria* to describe another kind of freedom: liberty from sin and its corrosive control. This word signifies release from a jail-like existence into an expansive new life. The Old Testament picture of this is the release of the children of Israel from slavery in Egypt into a new life of serving God in Canaan.

●　●　●

Jesus declared the fact of universal bondage when He said, "Everyone who sins is a slave to sin" (John 8:34). Then He quickly added that if "the Son sets you free, you will be free indeed" (v. 36). *This* was His mission: "to proclaim freedom for the prisoners" (Luke 4:18). And *this* is the great hope of the gospel: faith in Jesus frees us from the impossible task of trying to earn God's favor—and also from every other enslaving idea or habit.

In Christ we are free from the penalty of sin—and also from its power. The One who called himself "the truth" (John 14:6) said, "You will know the truth, and the truth will set you free" (John 8:32)—free from hurts, addictions, and wrong ways of thinking.

●　●　●

Forget others for a moment. What about the person whose teeth you brush every night? Are *you* living in freedom?

Remember: The freedom Jesus brings isn't a freedom to do whatever we desire. As Paul explained, many of our desires, even as believers, are still fleshly (Galatians 5:17)! Rather, Jesus frees us from compulsive and destructive urges so that we can pursue the new, God-honoring desires He's placed within us. It's a freedom to serve Him and others! And to guide and strengthen us, He graciously gives us His Spirit (see chapter 71).

MYSTERY

A previously secret truth about the plans or purposes
of God revealed to one of His servants

The mystery was made known to me by revelation,
as I have written briefly. When you read this, you can perceive my insight
into the mystery of Christ. (EPHESIANS 3:3–4 ESV)

L ife is full of mysteries:

- Why do villains in movies, just before finishing off the
  hero, *always* feel the need to pause and deliver a long
  speech, thereby giving the hero's sidekick time to show
  up and save the day?
- If the plural of goose is geese, shouldn't the plural
  of moose be meese?
- Since jelly toast always lands face down, and cats always land feet first, what would happen if you strapped
  a piece of jelly toast to the back of your cat and shoved
  it off the refrigerator?[*]

The story of God contains mysteries too—much more signifi-
cant ones.

---

[*] If you try this fun little experiment, I'd love to hear how things come out. Email me at
lenwoods@gmail.com.

• • •

Our English word *mystery* comes straight from the Greek word *mystērion*. The word means "secret things." In the New Testament, however, it refers to God's previously secret purposes that He has chosen to reveal to select servants.

Six times in his short letter to the Christians at Ephesus, the apostle Paul used this term to speak of the mysterious plan or will of God (1:9) to bring Jews and Gentiles together into one body and make them co-heirs of all the riches of God (2:19). He also spoke of "the mystery of Christ" (3:4), the mystery of marriage (5:32), and "the mystery of the gospel" (6:19).

• • •

To be sure, not every spiritual mystery is revealed in the Bible. Deuteronomy 29:29 reminds us, "The secret things belong to the LORD our God."

This side of heaven we won't fully comprehend conundrums like these: how can God be three yet one, or how can Jesus be fully God and fully man, or why does a God who's all-powerful and all-good allow evil and suffering?

In truth, it's good that God doesn't pull back the curtains and reveal everything. If He did, our little brains would short-circuit and our hearts would explode.

• • •

The spiritual life is full of mysteries:

- How is it possible that Christ can actually live within us (Colossians 1:27)?
- Why would Jesus fiercely love (and be devoted to) faithless people such as us (Ephesians 5:31–32)?

- How, as redeemed sinners in a fallen world, can we possibly live godly lives (1 Timothy 3:16)?
- What will that day be like when we are forever changed (1 Corinthians 15:51)?

Since it's doubtful in this life that we'll fully comprehend such ineffable realities, maybe it's enough to shake our heads in wonder and lift our eyes heavenward with humility and gratitude.

GROW

The process of a person or thing slowly
reaching its potential

Instead, speaking the truth in love, we will grow to become in every
respect the mature body of him who is the head, that is, Christ.
(EPHESIANS 4:15)

The expectant mom rubs her growing belly and thinks about the eight-year-old girl in the back bedroom who is growing almost as fast as the weeds in the front garden. She shakes her head at the way her husband's company has grown from a start-up to a profitable business in just a few years' time (and how, during that span, he and his cofounder have grown weary of one another).

We would expect a ubiquitous word like *grow* to be found in the Bible. And it is. Pity the person who misses it.

• • •

Writing to first-century Christians in Ephesus, the apostle Paul first reviewed all that God has done to give us spiritual life (Ephesians 1–3). Then, in the second half of his letter (Ephesians 4–6), he focused on what spiritual growth looks like.

Paul used a Greek word that means "to increase."[*] In secular Greek this word was used to express the idea of attaining the

---

[*] *Auxano* is the Greek word translated "grow."

highest position. It refers to the process of a person or thing becoming all that it has within it to be, either good or bad. (Remember, a person can grow to be a saint—or a monster.)

Luke 2:52 notes that "Jesus grew in wisdom and stature, and in favor with God and man."

Other passages say we can grow in faith (2 Corinthians 10:15) and in the grace and knowledge of Jesus (2 Peter 3:18). With the right spiritual diet, we can grow in our understanding of our great salvation (1 Peter 2:2). By clinging to Jesus in faith, we can keep from growing weary (Hebrews 12:3) or seeing our love for Him grow cold (Matthew 24:12).

● ● ●

When preacher-types talk about "transformation into Christlikeness" and theologians write about "sanctification," they're referring to spiritual growth.

Remember that it's the nature of all healthy things to grow. When a child isn't gaining weight in those first few months, we call the doctor. When longtime Christians behave like spiritual infants instead of grown-ups, there's a problem.

● ● ●

The concept of growing spiritually is confusing to a lot of people. It needn't be. Here are a few truths:

- God is the ultimate cause of our growth (1 Corinthians 3:6–7); however . . .
- Growth doesn't happen automatically. You don't grow musically simply by putting a piano in your living room. But get a teacher to instruct you and faithfully practice what you're learning, and you *will* see progress.
- This same principle holds for the spiritual life. Keep drawing near to God in prayer. Keep reading—and

seeking (ideally with a group of others) to live out—
Christ's teachings. As you do, you will see your heart
begin to change.

- Remember that growth comes in spurts. It's seasonal.
In the same way that plants appear to be dead in the
winter, sometimes we don't *seem* to be growing. Hang
in there, spring is coming!

REJOICE

To express deep gladness or joy

Rejoice in the Lord always. I will say it again: Rejoice! (PHILIPPIANS 4:4)

Ask one hundred strangers to describe the Christians they know. Sadly, you might hear—among other things—adjectives like *somber* and *grim* more than words like *joyful* and *glad*.

Why? Why are so many Christians so serious and solemn? If the message of the Bible is true—and we Christians say it is—shouldn't we be walking celebrations? Why do we so often act like "sticks in the mud"? Why don't we rejoice more?

• • •

The command to "rejoice in the Lord always" comes from Philippians, a short letter written by the apostle Paul while he languished in a Roman jail cell. In this letter, Paul used the noun *joy* five times and the verb *rejoice* nine times!* These two words convey the idea of experiencing and expressing deep gladness regardless of external circumstances.

Despite being in the slammer, Paul made it clear he had ample reasons to rejoice.

---

*The verb *rejoice* is *chairo*; the noun *joy* is *chara*.

- The Philippian believers were his beloved partners in the gospel (1:3–5)!
- He was confident that God would complete the work He had begun in them (1:6)!
- He kept hearing stories about how God was using even his imprisonment to further the gospel (1:12–18)!

For three more chapters Paul listed reason after reason for his deep gladness. The more he rejoiced, the more intense his joy. And the greater his joy, the more he rejoiced!

• • •

We often think, rightly so, of God as wise and powerful and gracious. But the Bible also speaks of God as joyful. The Old Testament shows Him prescribing annual festivals meant to be joyous celebrations. It speaks of "the joy of the LORD" (Nehemiah 8:10) and even tells of God rejoicing over His ancient people "with shouts of joy" (Zephaniah 3:17 NASB).

The New Testament highlights the joy of Jesus (Luke 10:21; John 15:11; 17:13) and the joy of the Holy Spirit (Galatians 5:22; 1 Thessalonians 1:6). No wonder C. S. Lewis concluded, "Joy is the serious business of heaven."[*]

The fact is, when we rejoice as a way of life, we resemble the One in whose image we're made.

• • •

In commanding, "Always be joyful" (1 Thessalonians 5:16 NLT), Paul showed that joy is a choice, not simply a feeling. (Who has the power to order their emotions to come and go?)

---

[*] C. S. Lewis, *Letters to Malcolm: Chiefly on Prayer* (New York: Harcourt Brace Janovich, 1964), 93.

Joy is also a virtue. We can cultivate it. How? Consider: In the Bible, joy is always tied to God (see Psalms 16:11; 32:11; 64:10; 104:34; 126:3; Joel 2:23). And as Paul demonstrated in Philippians, the action of rejoicing is connected with the condition of joy. In other words, the more we focus on God and express joy, the more we'll experience joy. And vice versa.

84

FULLNESS

Completeness, something in its totality,
superabundance, or wealth

For God was pleased to have all his fullness dwell in him.

(COLOSSIANS 1:19)

Depending on the day, most people are full of . . . something. If not good ideas, motivation, energy, or hope, then full of themselves, hot air, mischief, baloney, or despair.

Near the end of the Bible, the apostle Paul addressed a radically different kind of fullness—one deserving of our time and attention.

• • •

Paul's letter to the Colossian* Christians seems to have been prompted by concerns over a new religious movement making inroads in the region (see Colossians 2:6–23). Eager to combat this strange amalgamation of Greek philosophy, Jewish legalism, and Eastern mysticism, Paul urged the Colossians to remember the supremacy and sufficiency of Christ.

His statement that God was pleased to have all His fullness dwell in Christ† (an idea repeated in Colossians 2:9) is astonishing.

---

*Colossae was an ancient city in Asia Minor, or what we know today as Turkey.
†The Greek word is *plērōma*.

This is the breathtaking assertion that the man Jesus Christ contains the full measure of God. Expressed another way, it means that all God is—God in His entirety, in His infinite completeness—lives permanently in Jesus.

If that's still fuzzy, we can say it even more succinctly: The man Jesus is God incarnate. Entirely God. Completely human.

• • •

After believers pick themselves up off the floor, the fact of Jesus Christ's divine fullness should fill them with joy. John exulted in the truth that "from his [Christ's] fullness we have all received, grace upon grace" (John 1:16 ESV). The idea is that, like waves at the beach, the grace just keeps coming.

Paul added that because of Christ's fullness,

1. we can "be filled with the knowledge of his will" (Colossians 1:9 ESV);
2. apostles like himself were able to present "the word of God in its fullness" (Colossians 1:25); and
3. believers have been given fullness in Christ (Colossians 2:9–10).

Peter called this "[participating] in the divine nature" (2 Peter 1:4). That phrase doesn't mean we somehow become divine. It does means that God in His kindness lets us share in all the overflowing richness and abundant goodness that fills Christ.

• • •

Maybe you feel absolutely empty today. Or maybe you're full—but full of all the wrong sorts of things: worry, regret, bitterness, pride, envy, lust, and so forth.

D. L. Moody said, "Before we pray that God would fill us, I believe we ought to pray that He would empty us. There must be an emptying before there can be a filling."[*]

This might be a good moment to ask the Lord to empty you of all the junk. Then ask Him to fill you with "all the fullness of God" (Ephesians 3:19).

If we're going to be full of something, let's be full of *that*.

[*] D. L. Moody, *Secret Power* (Albany, OR: Books for the Ages, AGES Software, USA Version 1.0, 1997), 18.

PRAY

To commune with God heart-to-heart

Pray continually. (1 Thessalonians 5:17)

The young executive returns from another grueling week on the road. Her young children swarm her, pawing at her bag. Of course! They want the little surprises she always brings them. Meanwhile, the woman's thankful husband swallows her up in a tight embrace. He could care less about some trinket—she's the real treasure.

A similar scene plays out daily in the lives of many believers. Rushing at God with a "Gimme, gimme!" mind-set, we can sometimes get so obsessed with His gifts, we forget that just being with Him is the real blessing.

Maybe we should spend a few moments reviewing the great Bible word *pray.*

• • •

In 1 Thessalonians 5:17—a verse anyone can memorize and everyone should—the apostle Paul uses the generic, all-encompassing term[*] for addressing God. *Pray* here can mean to make entreaties for others, to offer up requests for ourselves, to confess sin, express thanksgiving, and so on. Notice Paul says we are to do this "continually."

---

[*] *Pray* here is the common Greek verb *proseuchamai.*

His point is unmistakable: Prayer is an ongoing conversation with God (not an occasional monologue). Should we bring our needs and worries to God (Philippians 4:6–7)? Absolutely! But we don't treat the Lord like a heavenly vending machine. We give thanks. We enjoy His presence. We're open and honest with Him like we would be with a trusted friend.

We also listen. This is why it's wise to pray with our Bibles open. As we do, we're reminded of God's promises, and we hear His gentle, correcting voice. This kind of back-and-forth dialogue is how we come to know God intimately. C. S. Lewis hit the nail on the head when he observed that prayer changes us, not God.

● ● ●

Jesus taught His followers the Lord's Prayer (Matthew 6:9–13). This short petition is pure genius. Rather than a formula to memorize and repeat mindlessly, its words are meant to jog our hearts and serve as a broad outline for our praying. The prayer reminds us that

1. we have a Father in heaven who is wise and caring;
2. we should always wrap our prayers in a preeminent desire for God's glory and rule (both in our lives and in the world); and
3. we can bring all our physical needs and spiritual concerns to Him.

● ● ●

Some people (maybe you?) don't exactly feel competent when it comes to prayer. The whole experience can seem strange and awkward. No reason to stress. Prayer is like anything else. We learn to do it by doing it. The more we engage in it, the better we get at it, and the more natural it becomes.

BUSYBODIES

Those who spend their time focused on and
meddling in the lives of others

We hear that some among you are idle and disruptive.
They are not busy; they are busybodies. (2 THESSALONIANS 3:11)

Every week our eyes widen over another revelation about how government agencies and business entities are watching us and tracking our every move. But can we be honest? Thanks to Facebook, Instagram, and Twitter, we've been doing all that to one another for years.

On the various feeds of our assorted apps, we keep tabs daily on all sorts of people: a celebrity's "selfie du jour," a coworker's vacation, a neighbor's workout regimen, a stranger's lunches. (*Time* magazine reported back in late 2015 that Americans check their smartphones eight billion—with a *b*—times a day! Imagine what the figure is today.) Often, in the midst of all our checking, we stumble upon lively online discussions. Sometimes we jump in, uninvited, adding our thoughts to the mix.

All this is why we ought to pause and consider the obscure word *busybodies*, found just twice in the New Testament.

● ● ●

In two of his less well-known letters, the apostle Paul warned about busybodies. The Greek word Paul used in 2 Thessalonians 3:11 refers to one who meddles in the affairs of others, rather than staying busy doing productive things.*

In 1 Timothy 5:13, Paul employed a related word, except in that verse Paul painted the picture of a first-century idle person going house to house gossiping.

How quaint. Thanks to the information superhighway, we don't have go house to house—in fact, we don't have to leave our couch! We can click our way from website to website, from app to app. It's an intoxicating formula: The Internet + Social Media = Hours and Hours of Fun!

• • •

In a fascinating passage near the end of the gospel of John (21:18–22), the resurrected Jesus was talking to Peter about his future—and some hard times ahead. Peter saw John sitting there, and blurted out, "Lord, what about him?" Christ's reply was classic, "If I want him to remain alive until I return, what is that to you? You must follow me."

In other words, "Peter quit worrying about others and obsessing over *their* lives. Do the things I've called *you* to do."

• • •

The Bible's warning against being busybodies surely isn't a blanket condemnation of social media. We can use such technology for good.

However, when we get so busy gawking at the lives of others that we forget to live the life God has called us to live, when we

---

*The word in 2 Thessalonians 3:11 is *periergazomai*. In 1 Timothy 5:13, Paul employed a related word, *periergos*.

stick our noses and opinions in places where they're not welcome, when we get sucked into a mind-set of comparing and envying and trying to keep up with others—we have a problem.

If Jesus is Lord over all—and of course He is—that has to include not just time and space, but the time we spend in cyberspace.

FIGHT

To struggle and strain for victory

Fight the good fight of the faith. (1 Timothy 6:12)

Obviously, we knew we had to bring our A-game tonight and give 110 percent. Our backs were to the wall, it was win or go home, you know? So when we got down early, we just kept saying: if we stay focused, keep grinding, and leave it all on the field, good things will happen. Sure enough—we came out with the win."

How can we not be amused when athletes get utterly lost in Cliché Land? Underneath the avalanche of platitudes, we know what they're saying. Success in sports—really, in any endeavor—requires an all-out effort.

The apostle Paul, in a wise letter to his young protégé, Timothy, said the same thing: "Fight the good fight of the faith."

• • •

We get our English words *agony* and *agonizing* from *agon*, the Greek word translated "fight" in this verse. The idea, familiar to any athlete and every soldier, is one of struggle and strain. It's the idea of exerting one's self, with every fiber of one's being. As corny as it sounds, it *is* the idea of leaving it all on the field—or the battlefield.

237

• • •

Because Christ promised His followers supernatural peace (John 14:27; 16:33) and joy (John 15:11; 16:24), it's easy to assume that faith in Jesus leads to an easy life where we get to, metaphorically speaking, kick back and sip drinks with little umbrellas in them.

In truth, the spiritual life described in the New Testament is less like a commercial for a Caribbean beach resort and more like the opening scene of *Saving Private Ryan.**

Why? Why is the life of faith such a violent battle? Because we have an enemy (see chapter 29) who never takes a day off and who comes at us from every angle. Some days it's like trench warfare of the soul just trying to cling to faith (see chapter 97). Other times we have to engage in hand-to-hand combat with our own balky hearts just to take small steps of faith. Add fierce ambushes from a hostile culture. Throw in the fact that many attempts to gently share our faith are met with withering counterattacks.

It's a fight all right.

• • •

General William T. Sherman, of Civil War fame, was right: "War is hell." Which means fighting is never "fun." Notice, however, that Paul calls the fight of faith "good."

It's good to put on God's armor (see Ephesians 6) and engage in the all-important battle for souls—your own as well as the souls of those God has put around you.

As you do, it's also good to have a battalion of like-minded allies fighting and agonizing next to you. Do you have that? Find some people who will encourage you to stay focused, keep grinding, and leave it all on the (battle)field.

---

*This 1998 Oscar-winning movie—directed by Steven Spielberg and starring Tom Hanks—begins with a harrowing, hard-to-watch reenactment of the Allied invasion of Normandy on D-Day during World War II.

INSPIRED

Breathed out by God

All Scripture is inspired by God and profitable for teaching, for reproof, for correction, for training in righteousness. (2 TIMOTHY 3:16 NASB)

It's fun to browse in bookstores and read the blurbs publishers use to promote their latest books. Look—over there is a novel that's "Remarkable...a dazzling tour de force!" It's next to "A gritty page-turner that crackles with tension!" ... just below a bestseller hailed as "A towering achievement . . . an astonishing work . . . a modern-day masterpiece."

What about the Bible?

How does it describe itself?

Inspired.

• • •

Most scholars agree that 2 Timothy is the last letter the apostle Paul ever wrote. It's definitely his most personal correspondence: a wise old saint realizing he's at the end of the road, sharing a few final thoughts and encouragements with a beloved young protégé.

We would expect a man of God to focus on the word of God, and Paul does not disappoint. He states that even though *he* is locked up, "God's word is not chained" (2:9). Paul then urges his partner in the gospel to be a worker "who correctly handles the word of truth" (2:15) and, in closing, charges him to "Preach the word" (4:2).

Why such an emphasis on Scripture, Paul? Because it is "*inspired by God.*" The Greek word Paul used here means "God-breathed."* In other words—get this—God supernaturally superintended the various human authors of the biblical writings so that they wrote down precisely what He wanted to communicate to the world.

• • •

Understand that "inspiration" isn't the same thing as "inspiring"—lots of books are that. *Inspired* means that the biblical writings came to us from God (via Spirit-filled, Spirit-guided prophets, kings, priests, and apostles). And even though we no longer have those original documents, we have thousands of ancient manuscript copies. Thanks to the science of textual criticism, we can have complete confidence that the Bibles we read today are trustworthy. They reveal what God is like, and they show us what it looks like to trust and serve him.

• • •

At the risk of stating the obvious, the 101 Bible words featured in this slim volume make up only about .007 percent of the more than 14,000 unique Greek and Hebrew words God used to tell the story of the Bible. All those other words are inspired too, and worthy of our attention.

Here's a challenge: Commit to read the entire Bible, Genesis to Revelation, over the next year. It's not as tough as you think, and there are multiple ways to do it. One of the best is to use the YouVersion Bible app. It's got plans that will take you through the Bible in a year's time, reading just a few minutes every day.

---

*The word *inspired* is *theopneustos* in Greek.

Just think—a year from today, you could be able to say you've read every God-breathed word in both the Old and New Testaments. (And—bonus—when you get to heaven you won't have to worry about bumping into Malachi and having to admit you never got around to reading his book.)

HOPE

To wait with confident expectation

In the hope of eternal life, which God, who does not lie,
promised before the beginning of time. (TITUS 1:2)

Hope.
The mere word can make our hearts beat faster. And when
we manage to grab ahold of the gift itself, the effect is miraculous.
With hope we're able to keep going, even when all seems lost.

• • •

Depending on which English translation you've got, you'll find
the word *hope* some 150–200 times in the Bible. Old Testament
scholars translate multiple Hebrew words as "hope." Most of these
stem from a common root word that conveys the basic idea
of "trust" (see, for example, Psalm 71:5; Jeremiah 14:22).[*]

Another Hebrew word gets translated as both "hope" and
"wait"[†] (see Psalm 38:15; 42:5)—which is only fitting: don't hope
and waiting always go hand in hand? In the New Testament, the
primary Greek verb translated "hope"[‡] has the same sense: "to
look forward to with confidence; to wait expectantly."

---

[*] That word is *qawa*.
[†] That word is *yahal*.
[‡] That particular Greek verb is *elpizo*.

If you want a good snapshot of hope, check out those three kids sitting on the curb, each one clutching a fistful of change. What are they doing? They're waiting for the ice-cream man, of course.

It doesn't matter that they can't yet see his blue and yellow truck coming up the street. Never mind that they can't yet hear the loud, jangly music that announces his arrival in the neighborhood.

The children are sure he'll come. In fact, it never enters their minds that he might *not* show up. Why? Because he comes every Thursday without fail. And so they wait with confidence. And the waiting, though agonizing to ten-year-old taste buds, somehow makes the ice cream taste even better.

● ● ●

People often use the word *hope* when what they really mean is *wish*. For example, "I sure hope they call out my numbers in tonight's Powerball drawing." Sorry, but such sentiments are the antithesis of biblical hope. (You'd be better off trying to catch lightning in a bottle while you stroke your lucky rabbit's foot!)

Biblical hope isn't wishful (or delusional) thinking. On the contrary, it's rooted in the faithful character and flawless track record of God. Biblical hope, a sort of first cousin to faith, is the logical and confident expectation—even in dark and scary places—that God *will* make good on all His promises. Hope is what tethers us in life's storms. No wonder Hebrews 6:19 (NLT) says that "hope is a strong and trustworthy anchor for our souls."

● ● ●

Right now there's an alarming amount of bad stuff in the world (and perhaps in your own life). Biblical hope looks unblinkingly at all these grim realities, acknowledges them, and then—without any false bravado or naiveté—says, "Nevertheless, all *will* be well."

Ask God for hope. Then pay attention to His promises. Be still and listen. Do you hear hope's whisper? It goes something like this: "The story's not over. Keep waiting and watching. Trust!"

PEACE

Harmony and wholeness—life as God intended for it to be

Grace and peace to you from God our Father and the Lord Jesus Christ.
(PHILEMON 1:3)

While the apostle Paul was under house arrest in Rome (see Acts 28:16–30), he met a young man named Onesimus. Paul did what Paul always did—he shared the good news of new life in Christ with his new friend. Onesimus saw the light. He believed. His life was forever changed.

Only one small problem: Onesimus was, by Roman law, a criminal—a runaway slave, perhaps a thief too. In the mysterious plan of God, "it just so happened" that Paul was a friend of Onesimus's master, Philemon. Paul sent Onesimus back, with a letter of reference. More like a personal postcard than a formal epistle, Paul's note makes a stunning request.

It begins with a blessing, a prayer for peace (Philemon 1:3). Then in so many words, it encourages these two men, with ample reasons to feel hostile toward each other, to live in peace as brothers.

• • •

The New Testament word translated "peace"* is synonymous with the famous Hebrew word *shalom*. Words don't come any richer.

---

*The Greek word for *peace* is *eirene*.

Shalom conveys the idea of community and harmony, security and prosperity, blessing and joy. When *shalom* is present, there's health and well-being, satisfaction and rest.

True peace, the *shalom* of God, means much, much more than "we've temporarily stopped firing angry words or bullets at each other." Biblical peace isn't simply the absence of friction and fighting; it's the presence of all good things. The peace of God is life as God meant for it to be.

• • •

So much of our world is on high alert, and so many of our relationships are like powder kegs. Knowing that the tiniest spark might trigger an ugly and painful explosion, we often coexist—just barely. Joy? Harmony? Ha, more like 24-7 tension.

The gospel shows us a better way. The Bible tells the story of a heavenly peace initiative. The "God of peace" (Romans 15:33) sent a "Prince of Peace" (Isaiah 9:6) to offer heaven's enemies (Romans 5:10) "peace with God" (Romans 5:1). Those who accept God's terms discover a peace that's not only eternal, but also external and internal!

• • •

According to Jesus, the children of God get to be peacemakers (Matthew 5:9). According to the apostle Paul, when we're in a relationship that's marked by unresolved conflict, we are the ones called to take the initiative to make things right (Romans 12:18).

To what degree is your life marked by God's *shalom*? Where in your daily experience do you lack peace?

The Prince of Peace can make His home in us through faith (Ephesians 3:17). His Spirit can fill and animate our hearts. We can live a gospel life, one marked by peace (Galatians 5:22; Philippians 4:7).

Will we?

FAITH

Trust in God that propels a person to
live as He commands

Now faith is confidence in what we hope for and assurance
about what we do not see. (HEBREWS 11:1)

Talking about faith is easy. Babbling on about how we should all trust God, waxing eloquent about how belief in Jesus leads to blessing—let's be honest, a person could train a parrot to say such things. This is faith the theoretical concept (or maybe the smoke screen). Though this kind of "faith talk" sounds pious and impressive, it's a long way from biblical faith.

● ● ●

In the Bible, faith isn't merely a topic for discussion. It's a way of life, an animating force. In the New Testament, the Greek noun that gets translated "faith" is closely related to the verb that means "to believe."*

Thus, biblical faith means trusting God—not only inwardly and mentally, but also outwardly and physically. This kind of holy trust doesn't just nod at God's Word—it starts putting on its socks and shoes. It culminates in action. Though it begins in the hidden

---

*The noun *faith* is *pistis* in Greek. The verb *believe* is *pisteuo.*

depths of a person's soul, real faith eventually shows up on the surface of a person's life.

• • •

This is why Hebrews 11, the great "faith chapter" of the New Testament, celebrates all those faith-full Old Testament saints, not in terms of the religious doctrines they claimed to embrace, but in terms of what they did. (If you've never read that chapter, or haven't read it in a while, it deserves seven or eight minutes of your undivided attention. Grab your Bible. Then start reading and try to hang on.)

Notice how active—not passive—faith is. The writer of Hebrews says that it was "by faith" that Abel brought a sacrifice to God and that it was "by faith" that Noah built his famous ark. "By faith" Abraham . . . did what? Engaged in a robust Bible discussion? Pondered Job's provocative new memoir? No! "By faith" Abraham packed up his household after a holy, crazy dream and said farewell to his homeland. Do you see? Biblical faith isn't lemon squares and decaf coffee after choir practice. It's a holy adventure.

On and on the writer goes, with stories that make our hearts beat faster—or almost stop beating altogether. It was "by faith" that the parents of Moses hid their newborn son from a powerful, paranoid ruler. When that boy grew up, faith flooded his heart too, prompting him to leave his cushy life of privilege. Because of faith Moses chose to endure mistreatment with his fellow Hebrews.

Other giants of Jewish history, because they had a living and vital faith (or, more accurately, because it had *them*), "conquered kingdoms" and "shut the mouths of lions" (v. 33). Still others experienced the not-so-marketable side of faith: persecution and torture. For every faith-filled believer in history who has "escaped the edge of the sword," God only knows how many others have been "killed by the sword" (vv. 34, 37).

• • •

Faith, the supernatural ability to "see" the invisible, is a primary emphasis of the Bible. It's mentioned hundreds of times, and any third grader can see why. The original sin, the defiant act that unleashed evil on the world, was unbelief. When Adam and Eve refused to trust God, death took center stage. The whole world broke. Paradise was lost. It took Jesus, trusting God perfectly—and defeating sin and death through His crucifixion and resurrection—to make forgiveness and new life possible.

And if unbelief, a lack of faith, caused all the damage, then belief in Jesus is the only way back. No wonder Jesus was obsessed with seeing genuine faith spring up in the hearts and lives of His followers—always asking questions like, "Why did you doubt?" and "Where is your faith?" Hebrews 11:6 says it most succinctly: "Without faith it is impossible to please God."

The question is unavoidable. Do you have faith? Real, biblical faith? What do you believe—truly, deeply? It's easy to know. Look at your life—notice the things you do and don't do. Actions really do speak louder than words.

When it comes to faith, a person's behavior is the most accurate tell in the world.

PERSEVERANCE

The quality of patient endurance in the midst
of difficult circumstances

The testing of your faith produces perseverance. (JAMES 1:3)

When we witness exceptional people—a spellbinding speaker, a once-in-a-generation athlete, a freakishly talented singer—we shake our heads in awe.

What about when we meet someone who possesses the rare character quality of perseverance? How about that weary mom who is sixteen years into a lifetime assignment of caring for a special needs child? Or the single dad who has been working three part-time jobs since being laid off six months ago—and who just sent out resume #157?

Maybe those are the real wonders.

• • •

The Greek word most commonly translated "perseverance" in the New Testament means "endurance." It's the idea of patiently waiting, sticking it out, being steadfast.

We could define *perseverance* as a kind of holy stubbornness. It's opting to "remain under"* hard circumstances rather than run

---

* *Hypomone*, translated "perseverance," is closely related to a word composed of the prefix *hypo* (which means "under") and the verb *meno* (which means "to remain").

away from them. Persevering souls don't throw in the towel. They hang in there. They keep going—even when they're "done" and everything in them wants to yell, "I quit!" They consistently choose what's right over what's easy.

• • •

In a sense, the great story of God is one long story of perseverance. From one perspective, it shows the Almighty faithfully "hanging in there" with His fickle people. And on the flip side, it reveals weary saints standing firm even though on many days all they had to cling to was a few old promises that must have seemed either too good to be true or too distant to be of any real help.

In the nation's darkest moments, prophetic statements like "How blessed is he who keeps waiting" (Daniel 12:12 NASB) must have seemed like a cruel joke.

• • •

Writer E. L. Doctorow once compared writing a book to driving in the fog at night. He noted that you can only see as far as your headlights—but he added, "You can make the whole trip that way."

This idea applies to persevering too. We are sure to lose heart if we fixate on *when will these trials be behind me?* However, we can make it home when we focus on *what's right in front of me?*

If you're facing a hard situation and you're tired, resist the urge to dwell on what might happen next month or next year. Instead, strive to be faithful in this moment. Ask yourself, *What's required of me right now?* Then do that one thing.

SUFFER

To endure painful consequences or mistreatment

For it is better, if it is God's will, to suffer for doing good than for doing evil.
(1 PETER 3:17)

Problems. Traumas. Hurts. Difficulties. We could keep reeling off synonyms, but our word choice won't change this tough truth: suffering is unavoidable in a fallen world. No one is exempt.

Granted, that's *not* a very popular, fun-to-read message. Nevertheless, the Bible doesn't downplay this uncomfortable truth. As a matter of fact, God's Word doubles down on all the bleak talk. It says that people of faith, rather than getting a pass from all the pain, should count on an extra helping of heartache.

Yikes!

● ● ●

A handful of Hebrew and Greek words are translated "suffer" in our English Bibles. The word the apostle Peter employs thirteen times (yes, "lucky thirteen") in his first epistle was used in secular Greek literature to describe being hurt by the blows of fate or the disfavor of men or the gods. In the New Testament, this word often refers to Christ's sufferings. Peter used it here to speak of the afflictions believers can expect to face because of their faith in Christ.

To encourage those first-century believers who were facing persecution, Peter pointed to Jesus, the righteous one. When evil men "hurled their insults at him, he did not retaliate" and when He suffered unjustly (and unimaginably), He "entrusted himself to him who judges justly" (1 Peter 2:23).

According to Peter, Jesus is our example in suffering. When we take flak for our faith, we are to imitate him.

● ● ●

As much as we wish otherwise, we can't control how others treat us. We can only control how we respond. When people call us names online or act hateful in person, we don't get down on their level. Retaliation and revenge are not the marks of God's people. And speaking of "marks"...

Did you ever notice, in Mark's account of the suffering of Jesus, that the Lord was accused (15:4), flogged (15:15), struck and spit upon (15:19), mocked (15:31), crucified (15:20), and insulted some more (15:29, 32)? Ever notice what the centurion posted at the foot of the cross said after watching Christ suffer all these abuses: "Surely this man was the Son of God!" (15:39)?

Maybe when we face suffering the way Jesus did, we show onlookers that we're God's children too.

● ● ●

Suffering saints don't need a bunch of peppy platitudes. (If you're hurting and getting bombarded by such unhelpful remarks, I'm sorry; if you're thinking of sharing such glib expressions with a hurting friend, please don't.)

Consider how Peter ended his letter to suffering believers: "And the God of all grace, who called you to his eternal glory in Christ, after you have suffered a little while, will himself restore you and make you strong, firm and steadfast" (1 Peter 5:10).

That kind assurance doesn't take the pain away, but it does give us enough hope (see chapter 89) to take another step.

94

KNOWLEDGE

Awareness, understanding–and in relationships,
growing intimacy

Grace and peace be yours in abundance through the knowledge
of God and of Jesus our Lord. (2 PETER 1:2)

On a dating app, a twentysomething guy reads the bio of a young teacher with a dazzling smile. She's from Indiana and likes fish tacos. We could call this factual knowledge.

A week later on a get-acquainted lunch date, the young man watches the teacher from Indiana get teary-eyed while talking about one of her students. He discovers she has a quirky sense of humor. This is personal knowledge.

A year later, on their wedding night, the guy gets to know his new bride the way Adam "knew Eve" (Genesis 4:1 ESV). (But since people are not the least bit interested in this kind of knowledge, let's keep moving.)

Thirty years later, the two have become one. They know each other's histories and tendencies, likes and dislikes. They can often finish each other's sentences! This is intimacy at the deep heart level.

● ● ●

Life experience shows us that knowing someone can mean a lot of different things. The Bible says the same.

In Scripture, the word *knowledge* has a range of meanings. It can simply suggest an acquaintance with or awareness of someone or something (Genesis 29:5). But when Peter (see verse cited above) refers to "the knowledge of God and of Jesus our Lord," he's talking about something more: growing understanding and deepening comprehension. (And, yes, the verb *know* sometimes refers to the most intimate relations—as seen in 1 Kings 1:4; Matthew 1:25; Luke 1:34.)

• • •

Stunning, isn't it? All this means we don't have to settle for mere factual knowledge about God or a fifth-hand knowledge of Jesus—as we would if we were writing a paper about Alexander the Great. The claim of the Christian faith is that we can approach the risen Jesus, meet Him in a spiritual yet real way, and welcome Him into our lives (John 1:12). Through Christ we can get to know the triune God better and better (John 17:3; 2 Peter 3:18).

Even though this relationship looks different than every other relationship in life, it's no less real. The knowledge that Peter speaks of is knowing the God of the universe intimately.

• • •

People like to name-drop—that is, brag about whom they know. Typically, we roll our eyes. However, the Bible indicates that it's okay to drop God's name—provided we actually know Him.

In ancient Israel, when the people lost their way, the Lord spoke these words through the prophet Jeremiah: "Don't let the wise boast in their wisdom, or the powerful boast in their power, or the rich boast in their riches. But those who wish to boast should boast in this alone: that they truly know me" (Jeremiah 9:23–24 NLT).

We can know God through Jesus! That's the message of Peter—and the whole New Testament. But to do so, we have to draw near Him by faith.

LOVE

God's essential nature, personified in Jesus,
and available to us as a transforming, animating force

We love because he first loved us. (1 JOHN 4:19)

Great love stories never get old. Here's one of the best from the Bible:

Jesus calls two brothers to follow him. Turns out James and John are hotheads—ready to call down fire from heaven on anyone who gets in their way! Jesus gives them the unflattering nickname "sons of thunder" (Mark 3:17; see also Luke 9:54). But He doesn't give up on them. Nor is He worried. Petty anger is no match for His relentless grace.

Sure enough, after years of walking with the Lord, John's vengeful heart has vanished. In its place? A heart obsessed with—and possessed by—the love of Christ.

• • •

This son of thunder was so stunned that Christ would accept a person like him, he gave himself a new nickname: "the disciple whom Jesus loved" (John 13:23; 19:26; 20:2; 21:7, 20).

Love was all John could talk about.* In fact, almost a third of all the references to love in the New Testament are found in his writings.

---

*The Greek verb for this kind of sacrificial love is *agapao*.

In his first letter, John described this love our hearts were made by and for. He said it originates in God—because love is God's essential nature (4:8). It's lavish (3:1) and shocking—when we sinned, God responded by sending Jesus as a sacrifice (4:9). That's the selfless nature of divine love: it always seeks the good of the other (3:16). And the result? It's transformative (4:7–8).

John, of all people, would know.

• • •

So how do we become better at loving? John says we have to let God love us first (1 John 4:19). But of course! How can we express something we've never experienced? How can we show what we don't truly know? In his inspired words, we first have come to "know and rely on the love God has *for us*" (4:16, emphasis added).

This is the grandest promise and hardest-to-believe truth of all. No wonder the apostle Paul prayed that head-spinning prayer in Ephesians 3, that his readers might have the power to "know this love that surpasses knowledge" (v. 19).

Paul knew as John did that when God's love for us becomes real, everything shifts inside. No longer do we move through the world desperately looking for love. Confident that we already are loved—fully and forever—our entire focus changes. We turn outward.

• • •

If you could stand to be a better lover of God and people—and let's be honest, who couldn't?—do this: Open your heart right now to the One who loves you unconditionally. Do it for the first time—or maybe the ten thousandth.

Whatever your history, whatever your current situation, don't keep the One who is Love at arm's length for another second.

Hear the gospel again. Hear Jesus say, "Good news! Hot head, cold heart—it doesn't matter who you are or what you've been. I forgive you completely! And I love you forever! Stake your life on that. Define yourself as 'the one whom Jesus loves.' Then, overflowing with my love, move out into a love-starved world."

TRUTH

God's reliable nature, unwavering plan, and perfect will, revealed through both His written and living Word

I have no greater joy than to hear that my children are walking in the truth. (3 JOHN 4)

If it's information you want, there's never been a better time to be alive. In March of 2019, it was estimated that the internet contained some 5.5 billion pages.* Happy reading!

However, if it's truth you want, there's never been a trickier time to be alive. All those stats and stories, tweets and articles that come magically to our smartphones each day prompt the question: what of all this is true?

Each time we click or swipe, we encounter scholars and celebrities, politicians and religious leaders, reporters and marketers making claims and counterclaims. We know that data can be misinterpreted, or worse, manipulated. We know that stories can be fabricated. Thus, the rise of curious phrases like "alternative facts," "competing narratives," "fake news," and "your truth and my truth."

• • •

In 2 and 3 John—the two shortest "books" in the Bible—John used the word *truth* eleven times. Second John is essentially about

---

* According to https://www.worldwidewebsize.com/.

"deceivers" (v. 7) spreading bogus spiritual ideas. The apostle wants his friends who are "walking in the truth" (v. 4) to "continue in the teaching of Christ" (v. 9). Third John commends one leader who was living according to God's revealed truth—and calls out another who was not.

When we examine all of John's writings, it's clear that truth isn't merely a set of principles or precepts. Truth is a Person! God himself is truth (John 3:33; 17:3; 1 John 5:20). And God's Son is the embodiment of divine truth (John 1:14, 17; 14:6). Thus Jesus can claim to be the true light of God (John 1:9), the true bread from God (John 6:32), and the true vine who shares with believers the life that is in God (John 15:1).

For believers, living by the truth means living in a way that's consistent with Christ's life and teachings (2 John 9).

• • •

In our relativistic culture, you can have civil discussions about truth—IF you stick to the phrase "*my* truth" (and mention—about every third sentence—how "open-minded" you are). However, if you dare to speak of "*the* truth" (as in "Jesus"), the conversation is likely to go south quickly.

Two writers are worth listening to on this point. Flannery O'Connor correctly noted, "The truth does not change according to our ability to stomach it."[*] And G. K. Chesterton observed that an open mind, in itself, is worthless. We open our minds, he argued, for the same reason we open our mouths—to shut them on something solid.[†]

• • •

[*] Flannery O'Connor, *The Habit of Being: Letters of Flannery O'Connor* (New York: Farrar, Straus and Giroux, 1988), 100.

[†] G. K. Chesterton, *The Autobiography of G. K. Chesterton* (San Francisco: Ignatius Press, 2006), 217.

John's ancient readers didn't have "the cloud" or smartphones. Even so, they were inundated by false teachers! How much more careful do we need to be? Ask God to fill you with the Spirit of truth (John 14:17; 16:13). He alone can give us the power to live according *to* the truth and be witnesses *of* the truth (Acts 1:8) in a culture that's adrift in a sea of mendacity.

97

DOUBT

To have a lapse in faith

Be merciful to those who doubt. (JUDE 22)

Aren't you thankful for all those Bible stories that depict saints with bold faith? How inspiring to see people trust God in big ways!

On the flip side, aren't you secretly relieved (be honest!) when the Bible shows people struggling to trust God? Abraham, Miriam, David, John the Baptist, Peter—how encouraging to know that even "giants of the faith" have occasional bouts with doubt.

• • •

Jude—perhaps a shortened form of Judas,* the half brother of Jesus (Matthew 13:55; Mark 6:3)—wrote the New Testament letter that bears his name to believers in a culture filled with false teachers. With so many conflicting spiritual ideas circulating, many believers were having doubts about the gospel.

Jude's counsel was to shame such people, to hurl Bible verses at them like hand grenades and condemn them for their shaky faith, right?

---

* If you were a follower of Jesus named Judas—not the traitor Judas, but the other one—wouldn't you ask others to start calling you Jude (or Jay)? Just saying.

Wrong. He urged those strong in faith to "be merciful to those who doubt."

The word translated "doubt" here means "to separate or divide."* Here and elsewhere (Mark 11:23), it conveys the idea of a person who's got a divided mind and a heart wavering back and forth. (Fittingly, in James 1:6, the apostle James—also a half brother of Jesus—used this word to paint a picture of a doubting believer being like a wave that is "blown and tossed by the wind."†)

• • •

All the way through the Bible, the people of God struggled to believe. This doesn't mean they necessarily doubted God's existence. Often it meant they doubted His promises or power, His presence or protection.

John the Baptist, whom we've mentioned, is a prime example. He burst on the scene telling everyone within earshot that Jesus was the long-awaited Messiah (John 1:29, 35). But later, in a prison cell, he found himself drowning in doubt. He sent messengers to Jesus to ask, in so many words, "Was I wrong about you?" (Matthew 11:2–3).

John's example, like so many others in Scripture, reminds us that just because we find it easy to trust God today doesn't mean we will tomorrow. We often speak of "having faith" (or not). But since faith is more an action than an asset, more verb than noun, it's more accurate to talk about "exercising faith" (or not).

• • •

---

*For those keeping track at home, the Greek word for *doubt* is *diakrino*.

†Jude and James were eminently qualified to address the subject of doubt. It took them a long time to come to faith in their half brother Jesus. In fact, at one point they believed He was crazy, not the Christ. According to Mark's gospel, they said, "He is out of his mind" (Mark 3:21).

If your faith is wobbly right now, do four things:

1. Realize you're in good company.
2. Be merciful to yourself. (*Of course* you're going to have doubts. You're under construction, and God's not done with you yet!)
3. Ponder the question Jesus once asked Peter: "You of little faith . . . why did you doubt?" (Matthew 14:31).
4. Pray the succinct prayer the unnamed man in Mark 9:24 prayed: "I do believe; help my unbelief" (NASB).

98

EAT

To consume food

To the one who is victorious, I will give the right to eat from the tree of life, which is in the paradise of God. (REVELATION 2:7)

We are a generation of "foodies." Most folks can name more TV chefs than they can world leaders.

We finish lunch and immediately start thinking about dinner. Once upon a time we gave thanks before eating our food. Now we snap a picture of it and post it on social media for all the world to drool over.

Think maybe we have some "food issues"?

Maybe this is why eating is such a dominant theme in the Bible.

• • •

The final book of the Bible promises "victorious" believers they will one day be privileged to eat (literally "consume food") from "the tree of life" (Revelation 2:7). Alert Bible readers perk up at this promise. They remember that in the first book of the Bible God cut off human access to the tree of life. This was because Adam and Eve had eaten from another tree in Eden that was off limits—the tree of the knowledge of good and evil, essentially a tree of death. From that point forward, eating takes center stage in Scripture.

• • •

Before freeing the Hebrew people from Egypt, God instructed them to consume a commemorative meal of lamb, bitter herbs, and unleavened bread. At Sinai, He gave Israel numerous dietary restrictions. As the people of God wandered toward a land that flowed "with milk and honey," God miraculously fed them with "bread from heaven."

In the New Testament, Christ's first temptation—like Adam and Eve's—involved eating. Subsequent miracles included feeding the masses. The night before His crucifixion Jesus told His followers to remember His sacrificial death through the regular eating of a simple meal of bread and wine. Revelation says history will end with something called the "marriage supper of the Lamb" (19:9 ESV).

• • •

What other conclusions can we draw? Eating—like sexuality or handling money or interacting with one's neighbors—*is* a spiritual issue.

We do well to remember that God is the creator of carbohydrates and calories, fiber and fat, vegetables and vitamins. God is also the one who designed our digestive systems to break down food into the nutrients and energy our bodies need. Clearly, He intended for eating to be pleasurable—He didn't *have* to give us taste buds or make certain foods so delicious. But He did. He didn't *have* to center Israel's social/religious/cultural life around an annual series of feasts. But he did. Clearly, when we gratefully enjoy good food with those we love, God is pleased.

And yet, as with any gift of God—children, money, or sex, for example—we have to be careful. There's a fine line between appreciating food and being controlled by it or obsessed with it. It's when we look to food—instead of to God—for ultimate comfort or significance that we err.

Ask yourself regularly: *Why* do I eat *what* I eat *when* and *how* I eat it? Am I truly hungry—or just bored or nervous? Am I grateful?

The apostle Paul's counsel: always eat in such a way that God is glorified (1 Corinthians 10:31).

HEAVEN

The place where the triune God dwells with
His angels and the redeemed

Then I saw a new heaven and a new earth; for the first heaven and
the first earth passed away. (Revelation 21:1 nasb)

Every few months another book comes out about someone dying, visiting heaven briefly, then coming back to life. Every few years one of these books is made into a movie starring Greg Kinnear (or another actor who looks like him).

Christians are sharply divided on whether such heavenly excursions are real or imagined. Many don't believe that heaven actually hosts "open houses" (even though the apostle Paul *did* relate a story in 2 Corinthians 12 about being "caught up to the third heaven" (v. 2) and the final book of the Bible *does* document the apostle John's awesome glimpse of the life to come).

There is one fact nobody disputes: the great story of God culminates in a place called heaven.

• • •

In the Bible *heaven* sometimes refers to the sky above where clouds float (Psalm 147:8) and birds fly (Genesis 1:20), or to outer space where the stars twinkle (Genesis 26:4). More often, heaven is described as the place where God lives (1 Kings 8:30) and is enthroned (Isaiah 66:1). That's the case in John's remarkable vision we know as the book of Revelation.

One of the most interesting things about John's account is the way he struggled to find the words to describe the wonders he witnessed. "I heard a sound," he wrote (14:2). Then in short order, he described that sound as being "like the roar of rushing waters," "like a loud peal of thunder," and "like . . . harpists playing their harps." (Sixty-five times he was forced to resort to the inadequate word *like*.)

So many questions: Will eternity's playlist offer something other than harp music? Will we be able to fly around up in heaven? Is heaven actually "up"? Do all dogs go to heaven—or just the sweet, scruffy ones? The Bible is mum on such details, though John did witness an electrifying celebration (chapters 5, 7), a great feast (19:9), a final judgment (20:11–15), and a future filled with meaningful service and reigning with Christ (22:3, 5).

• • •

On the night before His crucifixion, Jesus told His followers, "My Father's house has many rooms; if that were not so, would I have told you that I am going there to prepare a place for you? And if I go and prepare a place for you, I will come back and take you to be with me that you also may be where I am" (John 14:2–3).

Maybe that's all we really need to know. Heaven is the home of our God. It's the place His Son, and our Savior, Jesus (an ex-carpenter, mind you—see Mark 6:3) has spent almost two thousand years preparing for our arrival!

• • •

Will heaven be spectacular? Beyond words! Yet the glory of any pearly gates or 24K gold streets will pale in comparison to the promise that we "will see his face" (Revelation 22:4).

And, in a way, we don't have to wait. When we eagerly seek the face of God here and now, we get little glimpses of heaven every now and then.

NEW

Better than what has come before

He who was seated on the throne said, "I am making everything new!"
(REVELATION 21:5)

A few months back a young couple bought the old dilapidated house on the corner. Then, in a whirlwind of creativity, craftsmanship, and sweat equity, they transformed the eyesore into a showplace.

Astonished neighbors can't stop gawking and gushing. This is a makeover for the ages. Sure, there might be some new home construction going on a few blocks east, but this total renovation is far more impressive. Turns out *new* is often just a synonym for *recent*. It doesn't always mean "better."

With one glaring exception . . .

• • •

Alert Bible readers point out that the adjective *new* pops up again and again in the book of Revelation. After his extended peek into heaven, the apostle John wrote about the faithful being giving new names (2:17) and about new songs being sung around the throne of God (5:9; 14:3). Ultimately, he described the wonders of "a new heaven and a new earth" (21:1), and a new Jerusalem (21:2) coming down from God. And the culmination of the great story of God? When John heard the one "who sits on the throne" announce, "Behold, I am making all things new" (21:5 NASB).

The Greek word translated "new" is *kainos*. It means new in its very nature, something fresh and different from the usual order of things. Something that is *kainos* is a remarkable upgrade over what has been. It's something wholly different, something much more impressive, attractive, or valuable.

• • •

In our fallen world, nothing stays new. That renovated house on the corner, the expensive car, the sleek smartphone, the designer dress—all these things get shabby and dated. All eventually need replacing. But the *kainos* of God means a day is coming when eternal freshness will inundate and permeate creation and swallow up forever the ancient curse of sin.

According to the Bible, *kainos* is the appointed end of human history. Through the prophets, God promised to do "a new thing" (Isaiah 43:19). Specifically, He pledged to enter into "a new covenant" with His people (Jeremiah 31:31). This miraculous arrangement would give all who believe "a new heart and . . . a new spirit" (Ezekiel 36:26). Jesus explained that this inner transformation is possible for anyone through a new (that is, spiritual) birth (John 3).

Apart from *kainos*, we remain stuck in old ways of thinking, enslaved to old ways of living (Ephesians 4:22). However, with the *kainos* of God, we are able to "walk in newness of life" (Romans 6:4 NASB).

• • •

If you have placed your faith in Christ, you are part of God's new creation (2 Corinthians 5:17). Not when you die, but right now! This means you get to do what a really good movie trailer does. By living out your faith, or as the apostle Paul put it, by putting on your new self (Ephesians 4:24), you get to give the world a faint preview of the dazzling glory that will one day envelop all things. Ask the One who is making all things new, to fill you today with His tantalizing *kainos*.

Since we *are* new, how about we live like it?

AMEN

"Certainly, that's true!"

The grace of the Lord Jesus be with God's people. Amen.
(REVELATION 22:21)

His message might be winding down, but the old preacher is wound *up*. "Do you see?" he thunders. "My brothers and sisters, do you see? The Lord will *often* make us wait...but He will *never* be too late!"

As if on cue, the rapt congregation erupts, the sanctuary filling with a spontaneous chorus of grunts, murmured yesses, and shouted "Amens."

Why do we say "Amen"—if not during a sermon, at least at the end of our prayers?

• • •

More than fifty times throughout the Bible, we find people blurting out this word—often twice in a row, for emphasis. Here's a fun linguistics fact you may not know: we get our English word *amen* from the Hebrew word *amen*. Imagine that.

So what does it mean? *Amen* is an expression of faith. It's an affirmation meaning "Truth!" or "Indeed!" or "May it be so!" Think of saying "Amen!" as a verbal rubber stamp. It's a way of seconding, or underlining and italicizing a spiritual sentiment. *Amen* is the teenager who says, "Totally!" and the accountant who says, "I concur," and the Jewish grandmother who mutters, "From your mouth to God's ear!"

• • •

Amen is closely related to the Hebrew verb *aman,* which means "to believe or support, to be certain or faithful." Two images are helpful: (1) a loving father cradling a newborn in his big strong arms; (2) a big government building with massive stone pillars and sturdy granite doorposts (see 2 Kings 18:16). Whatever we are "amen-ing" is like this: strong and trustworthy, reliable and dependable. Whatever is "amen-able" is a reality you can bank on, a certainty you can hang your hat on.

• • •

No wonder, then, that Jesus Christ himself is called "the Amen, the faithful and true witness" (Revelation 3:14). He is the ultimate divine "Yes!"—the sure and certain guarantor of all the plans and promises of God.

The Bible concludes fittingly with the word *Amen.* It's heaven's way of saying, "All you've just read in all these books—every single word—count on it!"

Amen?

Amen!

AFTERWORD

As I write the final words of this book about Bible words, March Madness (the NCAA hoops tournament) is getting underway. Like they do every year, some fans are fussing about "undeserving" teams that got invited to the big dance and "deserving" schools that got snubbed.

It occurs to me you might feel that way about this book—surprised that certain words were included, upset that others were left out. "You think *busybodies* is a more important word than *righteousness*?!" Or "*Records* made the cut, but *flesh* didn't?!"

That's the fun—and beauty—of a list. Whether it's the "64 Best Men's College Basketball Teams This Season," the "Ten Greatest Movies of All Time," or "101 Important Words About the Bible," lists force us to think—and rethink. Since they're inherently limiting and largely subjective, they always spark lively discussion.

The debates can continue indefinitely, but every list has to stop somewhere. So let's end this list of important Bible words with one last word—the word *Word*.

The apostle John began his gospel by writing, "In the beginning was the Word, and the Word was with God, and the Word was God" (John 1:1). A few verses later he declared, "The Word became human and made his home among us" (John 1:14 NLT).

One doesn't need a divinity degree to realize that John was talking about Jesus. So why not come right out and say that? Why bother using that mysterious title "the Word"?

A lot of rich Jewish theology and Greek philosophy aside, here's why: Words are for communication. When a weary mom says to her grunting toddler, "Use your words," she means, "Express yourself. Help me understand what you mean, what you want." Therein lies the power and practicality of words. They shed light. They clarify. Without words, we're left to wonder and guess. With them, the lights come on.

According to John, this is why Jesus came. As "the Word," He came to put an end to speculation about who God is and confusion about what God wants. Here's how John put it: This "unique One, who is himself God . . . He has revealed God to us" (John 1:18 NLT).

Thus, the word most worthy of our attention is this Word: Jesus. The other 101 words highlighted in this book? They're simply the language the Word used (and is using) to tell the greatest story ever.[*]

Remember, as we take those words to heart, we enter into God's grand story—and find that our lives are telling it too.

---

[*] Look for my next book *101 Important Words about Jesus: And the Remarkable Difference They Make* (Our Daily Bread Publishing, 2021).

DISCUSSION QUESTIONS

Suggested questions for book clubs

1. How do you think your peers, coworkers, neighbors, family members would describe the Bible? How would *you* describe it?
2. Did this book change how you view the Bible, and if so, how?
3. Is the idea of the Bible being a *story* a new concept to you?
4. The biblical writers used around 14,000 different words (originally writing in Greek, Hebrew, and Aramaic) to tell the story of God and the world. This book highlights only 101 of those words. Were there any important Bible words that you felt should have been included but were not?
5. What specific entries (words), if any:

   - Confused you? Explain how.
   - Made you angry? Explain why.
   - Helped you understand something you'd never quite grasped before? Explain.
   - Caused you to rethink some of your ideas or beliefs? Explain one of the changes.
   - Encouraged you? Explain how.

6. Do you have a favorite entry? Why do you think the discussion of this particular word resonated with you like it did?
7. What are one or two specific or practical takeaways for you from this book?

Suggested questions for small groups, Sunday school classes, or friends going through the book together

Note: *We suggest individuals read an entry a day on their own, then meet together weekly or every other week to discuss what they've read in the previous seven or fourteen days.*

1. God (Genesis)

What words come to your mind, and what emotions fill your heart when you hear the word God?

If two atheists were hiking and stumbled across the word "Help!" scrawled into the dirt trail, they would never consider that this "message" came about by chance, by a thunderstorm blowing branches and stones across the path. Why then do some people resist the idea that our complex world had an intelligent designer? Why do you think skeptics consider the universe the result of impersonal forces over eons of time—just a big, cosmic accident?

2. Make (Genesis)
What sorts of things do you like to *make*?

Do you agree that we humans are "natural born makers" because the ultimate Maker made us to resemble himself? Why or why not?

What's something you'd like to make *in the future*?

3. Die (Genesis)
The entry states: "The rebellion in Paradise is beyond tragic. The first book of the Bible opens with life in all its pristine beauty and marvelous goodness. Eden is a deathless world, just as God meant for it to be. But sin comes crashing into the picture, and as a result, Genesis concludes with talk of embalming fluid, coffins, and burial plots." What do you think about the idea that death (physical and spiritual) is the result of sin (that is, humanity turning away from the one true God, the source of life)?

4. Abraham (Genesis)
The writer used the image of an Old Testament "Mount Rushmore" of faith and suggested that Abraham, Moses (chapter 6), and David (chapter 21) would be the obvious first three choices. Do you agree? Why or why not?

Why is *Abraham* such a towering figure in the Bible?

5. Bless (Genesis)
The word *bless* means to give what is good. What are some of the ways God has blessed you?

What are some of the ways you can bless God?

6. Moses (Exodus)
From what you know of Moses's life, what stands out to you most? Why?

If you could ask *Moses* any question, what would it be?

7. Law (Exodus)
How would you explain the purpose of the Old Testament *law* to a modern skeptic who calls it archaic and primitive?

8. Tabernacle (Exodus)
How does the Old Testament account of God dwelling in a tent strike you?

Why do you think John used the Greek word for *tabernacle* when describing the coming of Jesus (see John 1:14)?

9. Holy (Leviticus)
The entry encourages the reader to ask this question: "Since the divine command to the ancient Jews—"Be holy because I, the LORD your God, am holy" (Leviticus 19:2)—is repeated to New Testament believers—"Be holy in all you do" (1 Peter 1:15)—how does holiness need to be part of the story I am telling with my life today?" How would you answer that?

10. Atonement (Leviticus)
What does the term *atonement* mean, and why does it matter?

11. Priest (Leviticus)
When you hear the word *priest* what do you think?

How do you feel about the fact that the New Testament says all believers in Jesus are *priests* (1 Peter 2:5)?

12. Rebel (Numbers)
What does it mean to *rebel* against God—and how is this different than "making a mistake"?

13. Cling (Deuteronomy)
Why is *cling* such an important Bible word?

What would "clinging to God" look like in your actual daily life?

14. Remember (Deuteronomy)
Why do you think it is so easy to forget really important things?

Do you think there is such a thing as "spiritual dementia"?

What are some spiritual truths you desperately need to *remember*?

15. Land (Joshua)
What does the word *land* typically mean in the Old Testament?

Considering your own "spiritual geography," what places hold your most precious spiritual memories?

16. Rest (Joshua)
What goes through your mind when you hear the word *rest*?

Why do you think so many people—including many Christians—are so rest-less?

17. Judges (Judges)
The time of the Judges (in Israel's history) was described this way: "In those days Israel had no king; everyone did as they saw fit" (Judges 21:25). In what ways—if any—does that mindset describe modern culture?

18. Kinsman-Redeemer (Ruth)
How does the story of Ruth foreshadow the coming of Jesus?

19. Prophet (1 Samuel)
What exactly is a *prophet*, and what important role did these figures play in the ancient story of God?

When, if ever, have you felt God calling you to say hard things to someone else?

20. King (1 Samuel)
The Bible says repeatedly that God is "the King of the earth." What about in your life? Is the Lord the true king of every part of *your* heart? If not, what keeps you from bowing to His authority?

21. David (2 Samuel)
What would you consider David's greatest accomplishments and biggest failures?

What qualities in David's life do you wish you could emulate?

22. Temple (1 Kings)
What's your response to the New Testament idea that believers (and not brick-and-mortar buildings) are where God dwells today?

23. Walk (2 Kings)
Why do you think the Bible refers to the spiritual life as a "walk," or as "walking with God"? What does that phrase even mean? How does one do that?

24. Records (1 Chronicles)
An overlooked truth from the Old Testament book of 1 Chronicles is that "God keeps records," that He is well aware of who does what. How does that fact hit you? How does it challenge or concern or motivate you?

25. Exile (2 Chronicles)
Why and how is the historical fact of the Jewish *exile* such a powerful spiritual symbol?

26. Remnant (Ezra)
Why do you think God makes such a big deal of small things, like *remnants*?

27. Awesome (Nehemiah)
Some Christians complain we overuse the word *awesome* ... that when everything is awesome, nothing is. Do you agree or not? What does it mean that God is *awesome*?

28. Enemies (Esther)
What do you suppose prompts some people or groups to be so vehemently/viciously/violently opposed to God, His plans, and His people?

29. Satan (Job)
What is your response to the biblical teaching regarding *Satan*?

If you believe Satan is just a figurative title for evil, how do you account for the fact that Jesus seemed to regard him as a real being?

30. Answer (Job)
What are the big questions you're asking right now—and what big answers are you seeking in life?

Do you agree with the author's contention that some answers will elude us in this life?

31. Psalm (Psalms)
Do you have a favorite *psalm*? What about that ancient song resonates with you?

32. Keep (Psalms)
What is your takeaway from the idea that God is our "keeper," that we can trust Him to keep us?

33. Heart (Psalms)
The *heart* is a prominent theme in the Psalms (and, really, throughout the Bible). What does *heart* mean in the story of God, and why is it such a big deal? (Hint: See Proverbs 4:23.)

34. Hallelujah (Psalms)
The writer speaks of a "hallelujah lifestyle." What do you think that means and looks like?

35. Selah (Psalms)
Scholars aren't unanimous when it comes to the meaning of this obscure Hebrew word, but it possibly means to pause and reflect on some lofty, eternal truth. Why is that a good practice? Is it *your* practice?

36. Proverb (Proverbs)
Why is it important to remember that a *proverb* is generally a true observation about life and not an ironclad divine promise?

Most people love a punchy, memorable proverb. Do you have a favorite? One that sticks with you and guides you?

37. Wisdom (Proverbs)
What does the Bible mean by *wisdom*? How does this differ from intelligence? Why is wisdom such a rare commodity?

38. Fool (Proverbs)
How would you describe foolishness? And what would you say to a person who came to you and said, "I'm tired of living like a *fool*. How can I gain wisdom?"

39. Meaningless (Ecclesiastes)
Have you ever read the Old Testament book of Ecclesiastes? If so, what's your impression?

What is the key to a meaningful life (please, no "church answers"—don't say what you think you are supposed to say, say what you really think)?

40. Beloved (Song of Songs)
Why do you think God moved His people to write this "racy" love poem and include it among the Holy Scriptures?

The New Testament says believers are God's *beloved* (Romans 1:7 NKJV). Is that your experience?

41. Light (Isaiah)
What, metaphorically and spiritually, does *light* mean in the Bible?

42. Servant (Isaiah)
In what specific ways do the *servant* passages of Isaiah point to Jesus Christ?

What, specifically and practically, does it look like today for you to be a servant, to serve others?

43. Covenant (Jeremiah)
When someone breaks a promise, or goes back on his or her word, how do you typically respond?

44. Angry (Lamentations)
Does it bother you that God is sometimes described as being *angry*?

When is anger justified, and when is it not?

45. Glory (Ezekiel)
What's something about the *glory* of God that you learned from this short chapter?

46. Dream (Daniel)
Do you *dream*? What sorts of dreams?

The Bible shows God speaking to people via dreams, and missionaries in the Middle East report many Muslims having dreams in which Jesus appears and tells them "I am the way and the truth and the life" (see John 14:6). What do you think about all of this?

47. Changed (Hosea)
The Hebrew word describing God's heart as *changed* means torn or flipped upside down. This, the book of Hosea suggests, is how our sin affects God. How does that insight affect you?

48. Day (Joel)
Reading this quick entry about the biblical word *day*, what's your takeaway?

49. Hear (Amos)
How would you rate yourself when it comes to really hearing others? Listening to God?

How is biblical hearing different than acknowledging sound waves?

50. Pride (Obadiah)
Pride has to do with elevating one's self. Culture commends and recommends this. God's Word condemns it. Why?

51. Appointed (Jonah)
How does the short, fascinating book of Jonah show God involved in human affairs, and why should we care?

52. Justice (Micah)
What is biblical *justice*, and how much is *justice* on the front burner of your mind?

53. Jealous (Nahum)
When is it wrong to be *jealous*, and when is it healthy and right?

54. Woe (Habakkuk)
What are some things in culture that make you shake your head and cry "*Woe!*"? (Anything in your own life that is woe-worthy?)

55. Gather (Zephaniah)
This entry says: "If your life feels like a scattered mess today, take comfort in the truth that God is a Gatherer. He specializes in finding all the broken pieces and bringing them together into a beautiful whole." Does that encourage you? How so?

56. Stir Up (Haggai)
When in your life have you needed to be *stirred up* (jolted, jarred, roused awake)? How exactly did God do that?

57. Angel (Zechariah)
What, if any, new truth did you learn about *angels* from this short chapter?

58. How? (Malachi)
When, in your life, have you been filled with skeptical, jaded "*how*" questions for God?

59. Jesus (Matthew)
Jesus means "the LORD saves." What precise things or situations do you need saving from today?

60. Kingdom (Matthew)
How was the *kingdom* Jesus announced different from earthly kingdoms?

61. Hell (Matthew)
What five words describe your feelings about the biblical teaching on *hell*?

How does this chapter challenge you?

62. Disciple (Matthew)
Disciple is a good, old-fashioned church/Bible word. What does it mean? What is discipleship, and why is it for every believer in Christ?

63. Cross (Matthew)
Some point to the *cross* of Christ and say that, as symbols go, it's offensive and barbaric. What do you say in response?

Do you think it's wrong for people to turn the cross into a piece of jewelry?

64. Gospel (Mark)
How would you summarize the *gospel* of Jesus?

Why do you think so many Christians are so tight-lipped when it comes to sharing the good news of Christ?

65. Repent (Mark)
What do you think when you hear the word *repent*? What about the contention that repentance isn't primarily emotion (feeling badly about sin), but action—seeing the truth of God and submitting to it? That repentance is basically rethinking and redirecting your life?

66. Christ (Luke)
Can you explain what the term *Christ* means? (Go ahead . . . give it a try.)

67. Baptize (Luke)
What's the purpose of *baptism*? Is it a means of salvation, an illustration, an initiation, or a proclamation?

What's your own experience of baptism?

68. Lost (Luke)
Can you describe spiritual lostness?

What's the difference between being lost and not knowing it, and being *lost* and feeling it deeply?

69. Believe (John)
What are some "nonspiritual" things you *believe* deeply?

Why—really—do you hold the spiritual beliefs you do? What convinces you those things are true?

70. Life (John)
Ask yourself:

What in my life seems to be on *life* support—or maybe even dead —right now?

What if I invited the risen Christ to live in and through me today? What if I allowed His Spirit to animate me and empower me right now? What remarkable things might I see?

71. Abide (John)
Do you use the word *abide*? Spiritually speaking, is it your practice to *abide* in Christ?

72. Spirit (Acts)
What are your big, unanswered questions about the Holy *Spirit*?

73. Church (Acts)
What's been your *church* experience (the good, the bad, and the ugly)?

What are three things churches could do to improve their image to outsiders?

74. Apostles (Acts)
If you could have lunch with any three of the *apostles*, who would you want to eat a sandwich with, and why?

75. Paul (Acts)
What's something new you learned about the apostle *Paul* from this short chapter?

76. Sin (Romans)
How would you explain *sin* to a little kid?

Someone once said, "We're not sinners because we sin; we sin because we're sinners." What does this mean?

77. Grace (Romans)
What's something you need to take away from this quick peek at (or reminder of) *grace*?

78. Resurrection (1 Corinthians)
How is *resurrection* different than resuscitation?

What in your life could use God's resurrecting touch? Your faith in Christ? Your marriage? Your church? Your passion for your work? A friendship or relationship with a child?

79. Saint (2 Corinthians)
Is it hard for you to think of yourself as a *saint*? Why do you think?

How does this passage from the chapter strike you: "Because you are a saint, the desire to do right and to please God is always within you. You may not always *sense* that; that may not always *feel* true, but it *is* true. It has to be. In Christ, you're a new creature with a new nature. You're a living, breathing saint"?

80. Freedom (Galatians)
How does biblical *freedom* differ from culture's ideas about freedom?

How much are you living in true God-honoring freedom right now?

81. Mystery (Ephesians)
What biblical *mystery* baffles you most?

82. Grow (Ephesians)
What are some specific ways you've seen yourself *grow* spiritually since putting your faith in Christ? In what areas would you like to see more growth?

83. Rejoice (Philippians)
Do you typically wait until you "feel" joyful before you *rejoice*? Or you do find that by choosing to rejoice, you often begin to experience joy?

84. Fullness (Colossians)
In what specific ways does the biblical term *fullness* offer encouragement to a believer who feels empty and blah?

85. Pray (1 Thessalonians)
What, for you, is the hardest thing about learning to "*pray* continually" (as Paul commands in 1 Thessalonians 5:17)?

What's your current experience when it comes to praying?

86. Busybodies (2 Thessalonians)
How are the New Testament warnings to *busybodies* relevant today?

87. Fight (1 Timothy)
In what specific ways have you experienced the truth that the spiritual life is a *fight*?

What are the weapons and resources God gives to help us be victorious?

88. Inspired (2 Timothy)
What does it mean when Paul says, "All Scripture is *inspired* . . ."?

89. Hope (Titus)
What surprises you most about the biblical understanding of *hope*?

90. Peace (Philemon)
How is *peace* defined in this short chapter?

To what degree is your life marked by God's peace? In what parts of your daily experience do you lack peace?

91. Faith (Hebrews)
The writer says that *faith* is "holy trust" that "doesn't just nod at God's Word—it starts putting on its socks and shoes. It culminates in action. Though it begins in the hidden depths of a person's soul, real faith eventually shows up on the surface of a person's life." Do you agree with these thoughts? Why or why not? What's the biggest step of faith you've ever taken?

92. Perseverance (James)
How would you define *perseverance* for a third grader?

Who are some people you admire for their perseverance? (Have you told them?)

93. Suffer (1 Peter)
Suffering can be self-induced (from making foolish decisions), the product of living in a fallen, broken world (being the "innocent" victim of sickness or accidents), or it can come as a result of living out one's faith (persecution). Which kinds of suffering have you experienced most?

94. Knowledge (2 Peter)
How would you rate your *knowledge* of world events, the Bible, Christian theology, the triune God?

95. Love (1 John)
On a scale of 1–10, with 1 being "It just doesn't seem to penetrate" and

10 being "I am constantly undone and amazed," how deeply would you say you have experienced the *love* of God?

Why is it so hard for us to "know" the love of God in deep ways?

96. Truth (2 and 3 John)
How is a person supposed to know what's true in a culture with all sorts of competing *truth* claims?

97. Doubt (Jude)
Have you ever been through a season of *doubt* (doubting God's love for you, doubting if your faith was genuine)? How did you get through that time?

Why do some Christians get so angry at believers who are struggling to believe?

98. Eat (Revelation)
Why do you think food and eating play such a prominent role in the Bible?

What do you suppose Jesus thinks about our culture's obsession with food?

99. Heaven (Revelation)
What do you look forward to most about *heaven*?

What's a common idea about heaven that, best you can tell, doesn't fit with what the Bible says?

100. New (Revelation)
The final book of the Bible speaks repeatedly of all things becoming *new* at the end of this present life and world. What do you think about that? Does that excite you or make you uneasy?

101. Amen (Revelation)
The word *amen* is an affirmation of truth, a statement that something is firm or reliable. About what things in your life could you cry, "Amen!"?

ABOUT THE AUTHOR

A graduate of Louisiana State University and Dallas Theological Seminary, Len Woods was a pastor for more than twenty-five years. He's also been a butcher's assistant, waiter, chauffeur, and magazine editor. Now he spends his days helping individuals and organizations communicate important ideas. Len has authored or coauthored more than twenty books, most recently *Spiritual Life Hacks* (Harvest House), *The One Year Book of Best-Loved Bible Verses* (Tyndale), and *Who I Am in Christ* (Hendrickson/Rose Publishing). You can find out more at thewoodswords.com, the blog Len shares with his wife, Cindi.

INDEX